THE
scent of water

A COMPILIATION OF MOMENTS WITH GOD

Lynn Busby

Copyright © 2025 Lynn Busby.

All right reserved. No part of this book may be used or reproduced in any manner whatsoever without written permission, except in the case of brief quotations in critical articles and reviews. For more information, write to inscribepress @gmail.com.

Published by Inscribe Press, Hillsboro, Oregon.
Cover and interior design by Lynn Busby.
Cover art by Keisha Brown.
   (https://kelanieco.com/en-ca)

Unless otherwise indicated, Scripture quotations are from The ESV® Bible (The Holy Bible, English Standard Version®), © 2001 by Crossway, a publishing ministry of Good News Publishers. Used by permission. All rights reserved. Verses marked NIV taken from The Holy Bible, New International Version®, NIV®. Copyright © 1973, 1978, 1984, 2011 by Biblica, Inc. Used with permission of Zondervan. All rights reserved worldwide. www.zondervan.com. Verses marked NKJV taken from the New King James Version®. Copyright © 1982 by Thomas Nelson. Used by permission. All rights reserved. Verses marked (PME) are taken from the PHILLIPS MODERN ENGLISH BIBLE, by J. B. Phillips, "The New Testament in Modern English", Copyright© 1962 edition, published by HarperCollins.

Printed in the United States of America.
ISBN 978-1-951611-67-5

Dedication

This book is dedicated to the Lord, from whom all words flow and to whom all glory belongs.

In the beginning was the Word, and the Word was with God, and the Word was God" (John 1:1).

May these pages reflect His truth and draw every reader closer to Him.

Contents

Foreword / ix
Acknowledgments / xiii
Preface / 2
1) The Closet / 8
2) Unloved / 16
3) As it is in Heaven / 20
4) I Will Watch / 26
5) Grace Upon Grace / 30
6) Lens Matters / 34
7) Giants in the Land / 40
8) Kodachrome / 44
9) Where Have all the Fathers Gone? / 48
10) The Promise Keeper / 52
11) Mirror, Mirror / 58
12) A Sunday Buffet / 62
13) Drive-Through Devotional / 68
14) The Power of the Blood / 72
15) The Whisper / 76
16) Like the Dew / 80
17) I Choose You / 84
18) So Come / 90
19) Resting Place / 96
20) Stay / 100
21) Intimate / 104

22) God's Pocket / 108
23) Clark Kent / 114
24) Intercessors Wanted / 120
25) Ship Out of Water / 124
26) Honour / 130
27) Do You Want to be Important? / 136
28) The Necklace / 140
29) Singing Servant / 144
30) One Last Dream / 148
31) The Sand / 152

Foreword

From the very beginning of creation, God has spoken. He said: "let there be light" and it was so. He spoke order into primordial chaos. He created humans in His image and immediately began to walk and talk with them. Our Creator is not some distant, unapproachable, unknowable Power. He is loving and interactive. He cares about us and the world He placed us in, and on top of that, He *enjoys* us.

When you read the Scriptures, you can't get far without realizing that one of the ways God often communicated His will and His purposes to His servants was through dreams. And it wasn't only His people—He even spoke to those who did not know Him (Abimelech—Genesis 20:3-7; Pharoah's butler and baker—Genesis 40:5-22; Pharoah—Genesis 41:1-36; a Midianite soldier—Judges 7:13-15; Nebuchadnezzar—Daniel 2 & 4; Pilate's wife—Matthew 27:19). There are many more.

This mode of communication is one that seems mysterious to those of us less inclined to receive insight and direction from dreams. But our lives are, or at least should be, profoundly supernatural, and there are those individuals who still hear from our Lord in the night seasons, whether through dreams or visions, or both.

Lynn Busby is one of those individuals. I first met her through her writing and her fascinating accounts of the dreams God has given her. I was struck immediately by her humility and desire to learn what God was saying to her, and her willingness to obey Him. During our many interactions throughout the editing and designing of this book, I have found Lynn delightful to work with. She seems to me to be one of the unknown artisans that wander among us—a person who is profoundly "regular" in outward appearances. But *regular* does not mean insignificant or boring. Her dreams, and the rich inner life connected with them, is certainly anything but boring.

I am always impressed when I come across a person who is not overly impressed with themselves but is instead focused on giving glory to our Savior. Sadly, too often in the Christian world we see a desire for attention and notoriety, where too many of us jostle to be noticed and not-so-covertly seek honor from each other, desiring acknowledgment for our piety and godliness. Yeshua soundly rebuked that attitude when He said,

> *"I have come in my Father's name, and you do not receive me. If another comes in his own name, you will receive him. How can you believe, when you receive glory from one another and do not seek the glory that comes from the only God?" (John 5:43-44)*

Foreword

I believe Lynn is a quiet, unassuming daughter of God, to whom He trusts many beautiful insights and profound nuggets of wisdom. I suppose, if that is what it means to be "regular," count me in!

I had the blessing of working with her the past several months, editing her simple recounting of unique dreams and encounters with Holy Spirit and the wisdom she has gleaned. I tried to not dilute the childlike trust, wonder, and playful humor she exhibits in her writing, and during this time I have grown to appreciate her as a unique gift to the body of Christ. It amazes me how simple, hidden voices speak powerfully when our Lord chooses to reveal them, leting the rest of us know what He has been doing in the secret place with His secret ones who are secretly faithful. When He does, we all benefit from the beauty revealed to hearts of uncompromised devotion, and we see new aspects of our breathtakingly beautiful and transcendentally creative Lord.

Open the pages of this book and gain new insight into the wonder that is our ever-astonishing Creator. He has set a table and prepared a feast for us in the writings of Lynn Busby.

I am grateful to present them to you.

JEFFREY PELTON
Inscribe Press

Acknowledgments

To my daughter Angela and son-in-law Chris: thank you for being so supportive all these years. Nothing would have been possible without you. To my prayer partners: you prayed for me through doubt, and deadlines. To my friends who gave financial support: you literally put your money where my mouth is. This book might never have made it to print without your generosity. You are either angels or heroes in disguise. To Keisha Brown the contributing artist, thank you for your talent and love and dedication to God. To my editor, and publisher, Jeffrey Pelton. What do you say to a man who is a wordsmith? Thank you for your charitable foreword, and sensitive coaching through this challenging labour of love to bring this book to fruition.

And above all, to God: the Author and Finisher of my faith. The dreams, the words, the lessons, all flowed from You—may this bring glory to Your Name.

Job 14 7-8 "At least there is hope for a tree: If it is cut down, it will sprout again, and its new shoots will not fail. Its roots may grow old in the ground, and its stump dies in the soil, yet it will bud and put forth shoots like a plant at the scent of water."

Petrichor:

Rain itself has no scent. But moments before a rain event, an "earthy" scent known as petrichor permeates the air. People call it musky, fresh – pleasant.

This marvelous fragrance comes from the moistening of the ground.

Preface

The whole creation is on tiptoe to see
the wonderful sight of the sons of God
coming into their own.
(Romans 8:19, PME)

This was my dream:

I place a weighty book—so big I can hardly lift it—onto a podium. I understand it to contain the preface of the Bible. I anxiously read it aloud to a crowd of people who sit breathlessly on the edge of their seats. There is a sense of wonder pervading the dream as I wake up.

I wake with a sense of awe, although I am a bit confused. Who reads the preface of a book in public?

Who would ever be on the edge of their seat in anticipation of a foreword being read, let alone one bigger than a thesaurus and Strong's Concordance put together? If such a book exists, it would be a book about God, for sure.

Do not get the wrong idea. I do not think in a million years that I have, or will receive, extra-biblical revelation. So first, let's examine the noteworthy features of the dream.

What stands out, and the first thing I want to study, is "the preface." The difference between a preface and a foreword is essential.

Someone other than the author writes a foreword,

usually someone eminent, lending it credibility. **The preface is written by the author**; it deals with the genesis, purpose, limitations, and scope of the book and may include acknowledgments of indebtedness. It introduces the book's subject and supplements the text by indicating a point of view to be adopted by the reader.

As I considered the previous sentence, my heart leaped a little. God wants me to understand His heart as I read. He wants me to understand the purpose's genesis from beginning to end. This is a principle of biblical study: that we understand it is God's revelation of Himself to us.

I can relate to this. Keep the main thing, the main thing. For me, the main thing, consistent from beginning to end, is God's revelation that He desires to be *with* His people, both Jew and Gentile. To *be* our God. What does that mean? To be present with us, to be active in our lives, to be our provider, to be the One we listen to and obey.

Here is one of my favorite passages:

Be appalled, O heavens, at this, and shudder, be very desolate," declares the L<small>ORD</small>. *"For My people have committed two evils: They have forsaken Me, The fountain of living waters, To hew for themselves cisterns, Broken cisterns that can hold no water."*
(Jeremiah 12:12-13)

Do you know what I hear in those verses? Longing. He *wants* to be our living waters.

Preface

His anger at sin is not so much because we broke the rules. His heartache is our lack of desire for a relationship with Him.

I heard His voice whisper this morning the well-known idiom: "Your argument cannot hold water."

Any lifestyle created seeking fulfillment outside of a relationship with this loving God is an argument *that does not hold water*. We live in just the same way as those in biblical times who carved their own wooden idols. We worship dead wood; things that cannot answer us.

The application of this dream is simple and profound. When you read the Bible, remember the preface. The author (God) wants you, the reader, to adopt this lens when reading His word.

Understand that everything circles back to the realization that God *wants* to have His own people because of His great love. God has revealed Himself to us in diverse ways. I authored this book to contribute my piece.

We each have a unique perspective we offer the Body of Christ. I have been vulnerable in sharing, even the things God has shown me that were painful, and it is only a tiny piece of the revelation of God. But it is how God has revealed Himself to me. That is all each of us must share. None of us have the whole counsel of the Almighty.

That is why we need to keep reading the Word of

God, the Bible, to renew our minds. All our encounters must agree and align with the established revelation of God as He gave us in the Scriptures. As I already mentioned, we must listen to each other's point of view. We are not invited to possess perfect knowledge, but to constantly return to Him. Each revelation is a puzzle piece; however partial, each is a testimony to the God who takes delight in revealing Himself and His love in our ordinary lives, to enable us to bless the lives of others. All our encounters and revelations from Him must change our hearts and cause us to surrender to Him who is THE Truth, the Way, and the Life.

It has been the most exciting thing in my life coming to know Him.

Chapter 1

The Closet

The voice of the Lord is over the waters ;
the God of glory thunders ;
the Lord is over many waters.
The voice of the Lord is powerful ;
the voice of the Lord is full of majesty .
(Psalm 29: 3-4)

One of my first encounters with God.

The humidity of August closes in on a small bungalow. A young girl lies on her bed in a tank top and shorts, with a fan going. She wipes the sweat off her forehead and considers the day ahead. She must plan. Where will she escape to today? She imagines herself riding to the lake on her bicycle before the crowds gather. Maybe.

Or should she call her friend Maureen? The two of them could take a longer ride out of town. She imagines the effort needed to pedal that far and how good it might feel to put distance from her feelings. Not that she could explain it that way, but she feels the anger might fall off her when she grinds out in her bike chain, and she would feel better.

She stares at the door of her closet, her eyes closing in on the grain of the wood. She thinks about the peace that she seeks when she hides there when the fear is overwhelming. The fear makes her shiver, but she does not need to go there today. It is quiet in the house, and she is safe.

She walks to the kitchen, and is surprised to find her father sitting soundlessly. She can usually tell when someone is there. She feels a flutter of disappointment.

Instead of making a sandwich to take with her on a ride, she pushes the screen door open, calling, "Bye, Dad, going for a ride."

She feels free pedaling down the street, making her own wind. Instead of heading down the hill to the water, she turns left toward the main drag. She slows, the heat stifling her like a moist blanket.

It is somehow oppressive and comforting at the same time.

She meanders up and down the few streets of the town. Something makes her stop at the church on King Street. Straddling her bike and staring at the tower, she senses an invitation.

She knows the building; they go there every Sunday and she considers it a safe, if boring, place.

She hops off her blue bike and props it against the building, running her hand briefly over the rough brick. It is Saturday, and she knows the large wooden and iron doors at the front will be locked. She approaches the side door that leads to the basement. The latch pushes down quickly, and she goes in.

Her nostrils sting as she breathes in the strong, musty smell, which becomes overwhelming as she descends the stairs, but she feels a sense of adventure. This is a familiar place, but this time, she can look anywhere she wants! She stares at the grey concrete floor and knows it will be cold, so she removes her shoes. She has no desire to turn on the lights.

The large room that usually holds tables for the

annual Christmas dinner is empty. As she looks around, her eyes focus on a small door. She has never gone in there before. Her heart beating faster, she walks up to the door and opened it. It is a tiny room and the few items housed there fill up most of the space. She takes stock of the maintenance and cleaning supplies, wash bucket and mop, and stepladder. Her intense green eyes land on a wooden chair, and she wonders what it is doing there. Indeed, no one would want to sit in such a small space.

But she does! She thinks of her closet at home and wants to know what virtues this closet has to offer.

She sits gingerly at first, then slowly pushes herself against the stiff back. The closet is dark, but she is not afraid. Her pulse slows, peace gradually moving down her body with a feeling of smoothness, like honey.

As she rests, it seems the room is becoming brighter moment by moment. Are her eyes becoming accustomed to the dark, or is there now more light available in the space? She watches in wonder as light gathers and expands in front of her. She suddenly notices a painting. Is it a painting?

No, this is really happening. A man in a white robe is standing in front of her, and he is made of the light.

A combination of fear, awe, and love floods her senses as the most beautiful person she has ever seen appears before her. She is overwhelmed by the love flooding the room and her heart. It feels like she is floating or flying, completely weightless. Her chest expands as if holding the universe. She is surrounded and held up by this all-encompassing sensation of being loved. In the closet. The closet of her heart where no one is allowed. Where she is closed off. Safe.

But lonely. A need to respond feels like a blade of grass suddenly pushing through and appearing above ground. It grew as the fluttering expanded in her chest.

She does not know what to do or say as the presence takes over this small room. She slides off the chair down to her knees. The light is so bright, saturating her and the air around her. She hears, from the midst of the light, "Jesus."

"I am Jesus. I stand at the door and knock. Just say yes and open the door."

She had not known she had such a precious private closet within her that she could choose to open. Or decide not to. Amazement dawns: what seems like a thousand thoughts at once.

"God is real!" And even more astonishing, "God is here! Right now! Loving me and asking me to love Him back!"

Did she say yes out loud? She thought she had, but she could not hear anymore because there is a roar in her ears like an ocean. There is so much noise at one time!

The Closet

Layers and layers of sound, like waters, bubbling brooks, streams, currents, and waves, all seem to harmonize like a beautiful symphony! Every note on the scale at once and in every possible combination.

The waves of song crash over her, becoming louder, and it feels like angels are also in the closet. Time doesn't exist in this place, so she doesn't know how long she stays there. When she feels composed enough to do so, she leaves the closet. Noting the cold floor on her feet again as she crosses the room in the cool dark, she tries to understand what just happened. She feels strange, as if she is new to her body. It moves slowly, and her legs tremble like Jell-O. Her lips also tremble, and she feels weak. Up the stairs she staggers, and out the door, into sunshine so bright she is momentarily blinded. Her hands shake as she reaches for her bike. Walking it away from the building she can't think. She can only feel. That immense love makes her feel as though the bright sunlight is inside her. She feels like a completely different person.

It feels like too much effort to climb on her bike so she continues to walk it up the street, the bike providing something to support her trembling body. She knows she will never be the same.

That day is still vivid in her memory, marking a differentiation of life before and after this event. Stories can be told about this young girl and the spiritual journey that began on that sweltering summer day.

She is now a Christian.

That girl was me.

Ezekiel 43:1 Then he led me to the gate facing east; and behold, the glory of the God of Israel was coming from the way of the east. And His voice was like the sound of many waters at once, and it shone from His glory. And it was like the appearance of the vision I saw, like the vision I saw when He came to destroy the city. And the visions were like those I saw by the river Chebar, and I fell on my face. And the glory of the Lord entered the house by way of the gate facing east. And the Spirit lifted me up and brought me into the inner courtyard; behold, the Lord's glory filled the house.

Chapter 2

Unloved

> The Gentiles shall see your righteousness, and all kings your glory. You shall be called by a new name, which the mouth of the Lord will name. You shall also be a crown of glory in the hand of the Lord, and a royal diadem in the hand of your God. You shall no longer be termed Forsaken, nor shall your land anymore be termed Desolate; but you shall be called Hephzibah (my delight is in her) and your land Beulah (bride); for the Lord delights in you, and your land shall be married.
> (Isaiah 62:2-4)

There was a woman whose name no one knew, but everyone recognized.

Unloved. Unloved, she whispered to herself and the air around her.

People would walk by, try to catch her eye and smile, but she remained hidden, trapped behind her name—Unloved.

Until one day, she stared at the back of a would-be friend leaving, light dawned.

She called out, wanting her cry to tap that one on the shoulder, to call them back to her. If only those who reach could touch. The person disappeared. But something had changed. She knew that person genuinely desired to understand and change her name.

She allowed this realization to touch her heart; a transformation that was almost like magic occurred. She looked down at her chest, feeling something there. It was warm. It was now alive. She placed her hand on her heart and whispered, "Loved."

"Loved," she declared, first to herself, and then to the air around her, "LOVED!"

She threw her head back, stretched her arms to the sides, and shouted, "LOVED!"

She looked longingly in the direction of the one, the person who had changed her life, but they had gone. It was too late to return what had been freely given, so she would try to catch someone else's eye and smile. She searched others' faces, looking to make that connection again so she could change someone else's name.

This story is in memory of a friend.

Chapter 3

As it is in Heaven

Pray then like this:
"Our Father in heaven, hallowed be your name.
Your kingdom come, your will be done,
on earth as it is in heaven." (Matthew 6: 9-10)

As I worship this morning, I sing, "As it is in Heaven, so it is in me." It feels so personal.

I go into an encounter and revelation of the light of God's glory as it is in Heaven. I can find no darkness in Heaven. None. Nothing can touch me there—no demonic influence of condemnation or depression. No arthritis, no pain in my body. Absolutely nothing negative exists there. It isn't easy to articulate such a revelation as the one of glory. It starts with a lightness and an incredible sense of well-being! A bright light blinds me, and in my mouth I sense a slightly sweet taste. I feel a weight landing on me that grows heavier and becomes overwhelming. The weight and imposing Presence of God glue me to my chair. And I begin quivering.

I have a vision of myself prostrate on the floor before His throne.

No flesh can stand in His Presence.

No darkness can be found in His Presence.

No arthritis, back pain, headache, stress, fear, condemnation, insecurity.

The love of God is so pervasive nothing else exists. I am swallowed up in love and light. I am being held by a power that will never let me go, and I will be here with Him forever.

I am not sure how long I stay there. Time disappears in Heaven.

Eventually, I "come to" a sense of myself again. I am still sitting where I began worshipping, but I feel as though I have been away. I remain in the chair, feeling a need to recuperate from something. I am spent. I slowly take inventory of my body, moving each part, connecting with them again.

Then the Holy Spirit reminds me of Romans 8:32:

For God has proved his love, giving us his greatest treasure, the gift of his Son. And since God freely offered him up as the sacrifice for us all, he certainly will not withhold from us anything else he has to give. Nothing in the universe can separate us from God's love. I am convinced that his love will triumph over death, life's troubles, fallen angels, or dark rulers in the heavens.

There it is in Scripture—the prophetic word made sure by the written Word. When present with the Lord, nothing comes between. Nothing should be able to separate me from this experience of God's Kingdom. Jesus prayed, "On earth as it is in Heaven." He includes you and me in that too.

He decrees in YOU as it is in Heaven.

Then the Lord whispers to me the word "Deposed." I know the word means overthrown, but I go to look it up anyway. I know the Lord wants to show me something or explain something when I hear just one word like that.

When we hear something from the Lord, we should always take it seriously!

Proverbs 25:2: It is the glory of God to conceal a thing,
but the glory of kings is to search out a thing.

We must stir the hunger. To he who has more shall be given. But he who has not even what he has will be taken from him. We must steward the mysteries of God. That means treating them seriously and doing all we can to understand, interpret, and apply what God tells us. The hungrier we are, the more we shall be filled.

So, I excitedly go to my laptop and read about the word depose.

Depose: overthrow, unseat, dethrone, topple, remove, supplant, displace, dismiss, oust, throw out, drum out, expel, eject; and my favorite: show someone the door!

Read these synonyms for depose again, but after each word, fill in the blank and insert the thing you struggle with. What makes you feel separated from God?

Remember that this has been done to fallen angels

and dark rulers in the heavens. Fill in the blank with whatever dark power tries to influence or subdue you.

Remind it that it has been deposed and put it under your feet.

Your Kingdom come; your will be done as it is in Heaven!

Where His Kingdom is, darkness is deposed!

I invite you to rigorously oppose any thought that try to set itself up against the knowledge of God.

Chapter 4

I Will Watch

As the eyes of servants look at
the hand of their master,
as the eyes of a maid to
the hand of her mistress,
so our eyes look to the Lord our God,
until he is gracious to us
(Psalm 123:2)

I will stand on my guard post And station myself on the rampart, And I will keep watch to see what He will speak to me, And how I may reply when I am reproved. Then the Lord answered me and said, "Record the vision And inscribe it on tablets, that the one who reads it may run. (Habakkuk 2:1)

W*hy has Habakkuk* said he would wait to SEE what the Lord was **saying?** Why doesn›t he say that he will wait to HEAR what the Lord is speaking? God often speaks to His people through visions to give us understanding. A picture is worth a thousand words, right?

Also, in the Scriptures, He often asks, "What do you see?" For example:

The word of the Lord came to me saying, "What do you see, Jeremiah?" And I said, "I see a rod of an almond tree." Then the Lord said, "You have seen well, for I am watching over My word to perform it."
(Jeremiah 1:11-12)

God says HE will watch over His word to perform it. The Lord invites us to keep watch with Him. Both refer to a diligent, sharp eye to care for the sprout of the vision, the sprout of His fulfillment of the word happening. Remember Jesus healing the blind man: the first time He touched the man, He asked," What do you see?"

The man responded," I see men like trees walking." This makes me chuckle, because it is a good description of how our spiritual eyesight can be, especially at the beginning of our journey to hear God's voice.

Our vision can seem cloudy, and we are unsure what we see in the spirit. That is when you wait, and the Lord doesn't mind you asking, "What am I seeing?"

As we gain experience, we learn how to zero in our spiritual focus. Like a camera lens zooming in and then refocusing.

Interestingly, the image of an eagle has often represented prophetic gifting. An eagle can see its prey from five kilometers in the air and will not remove it's focus until the prey is caught.

We learn how to watch diligently for the word and the vision to be clear, and then we join with God to call it forward until it comes to life in the natural. We watch over His word with Him until it is performed. Another way we commonly refer to this is we are "pressing in" and "contending."

What a privilege and joy to see, to hear His voice and partner with Him.

How precious it is when we get just a glimmer of understanding of His ways.

Israel knew God's works, but Moses knew God's ways.

Chapter 5

Grace Upon Grace

"Now I commit you to God and to the word of his grace which can build you up and give you an inheritance among all those who are sanctified."
(Acts 20: 32)

"He will bring the capstone into place with shouts of 'Grace! Grace to it!'"
(Zechariah 4: 7)

I hear the Lord whisper, "Grace upon grace."
John 1:16 For of His fullness we have all received, and grace upon grace.

What does it mean to receive grace upon grace? Philo, a contemporary of the writer of the fourth gospel, in the first century AD wrote in *On the Posterity of Cain and His Exile*:

> After the first graces (τὰς πρώτας χάριτας), God bestows:
> other graces in place of those graces (ἑτέρας ἀντ' ἐκείνων)
> third graces in place of the second graces (τρίτας ἀντὶ τῶν δευτέρων)
> always new graces in place of the older graces (αἰεὶ νέας ἀντὶ παλαιοτέρων)
> yet sometimes different graces (τοτὲ μὲν διαφερούσας)
> but other times the same graces anew (τοτὲ δ' αὖ καὶ τὰς αὐτάς)
> or, on the one hand, the creature never lacks the benefit of God's graces since he would be utterly destroyed, yet he cannot bear an excellent and plentiful rush of them. Because God desires their use to benefit us, He measures the graces given in

proportion to the strength of those Who receive it. What does it mean to receive grace upon grace? For we have received of His fullness and grace upon grace. We receive grace after grace until the fullness of Him that we have received is realized in us as mature sons and daughters.

A picture comes to me. I see a stairway of stones in the middle of a gently flowing river going up into the sky. Somehow, I know every stone is grace. Each step could only be taken by faith.

Each step brings greater revelation of the immensity of God's grace. With each upward step there is an ability to walk in a more significant measure of gifting and calling.

Every stone ascended grants more remarkable courage to take another step. The understanding opens, blossoms in my awareness that the more we climb this stairway, the more grace we have, the more faith we have, the more faith we have, the more grace we and so on. Continuing upwards to the high call of God on our lives, we grow in faith to receive more grace, and then we have more grace to walk by faith. What does it mean to receive grace upon grace?

2 Peter 3:18 tells us to "grow in grace and in the knowledge of Christ our Lord and Saviour. To Him be the glory both now and to the day of eternity." The more we grow in the knowledge of our Lord (obedience) and Saviour (grace), the more we are whole and fulfilled.

Grace Upon Grace

This is what it means to receive grace upon grace.

These are simple thoughts on foundational principles, but sometimes we forget them.

We try to climb in our own strength.

Chapter 6

Lens Matters

"The lamp of the body is the eye. If therefore your eye is good, your whole body will be full of light. But if your eye is bad, your whole body will be full of darkness. If therefore the light that is in you is darkness, how great is that darkness!" (Matthew 6: 22-23)

When *people start* seeing visions, having dreams, and hearing God's voice, they want to tell everyone everything they hear. This is a natural response, because it is so exhilarating!

It was the same for me.

My pastor was kind and gracious, adopting a patient look when I would tell him the latest revelation I had received.

Others were not as compassionate.

I did not understand! Why was it not exciting to them, as well! But I kept pressing in to receive from the Lord. I matured, I heard more, and I learned more. In fact, the rejection I experienced worked in my favour. I turned to God when I was hurt and discouraged.

I entered the school of the prophets. Haha! Those of you in this school know why I insert a chuckle. There is nothing like being schooled by the Lord. His discipline reaches depths that mere words do not. He has a way of saying things that expose our hearts. I learned to be careful about complaining to the Lord!

Once, I asked the Lord why the people were not receiving a particular word.

The air around me grew still with the thick quiet that usually precedes a scalpel-like precise correction from the Lord.

"Did YOU receive it?" was the response.

That stillness that was at the same time disquieting surrounded me. "I am listening, Lord."

He went on, showing me how I was a blabber. Someone who "overshares thoughtlessly" That I did not take in words for myself first, allowing them to have a corrective work over my soul. He reminded me that He told His prophet to EAT the scrolls He gave them. His words of correction are sweet. But they have an edge to them. Sharper than a two-edged sword dividing between soul and spirit. It slices me open in a very clean way. Swiftly exposing heart motives without leaving shame in it's wake only clean conviction.

What we initially receive as prophetic people is meant to cleanse our hearts and clear the logs out of our own eyes before trying to help someone else. It must have its way in us, changing us first! That is biblical! See Matthew 7:3-5.

Prophetic gifting is often described as the eye of the body and sometimes I see it symbolized in my dreams by glasses and cameras. Night vision glasses are an excellent metaphor for the prophetic. Using this gift, we can see our enemies: where they are, and what they are up to.

Lens Matters

Have you heard of rose-colored glasses?

Whatever your outlook on life, your lens will affect how you view circumstances and events. It will also affect how you see things in the Spirit and influence how you speak the word of the Lord. A rose-colored perspective is one that refuses to acknowledge the balance of corrective words; instead, everything must always be upbeat and encouraging. The problem with a steady "diet" of these kinds of words is that they create a sort of "lullaby" affect. Soft like a blanket, they do not rouse us to transformation.

There are also dark shades of lenses. This is when you have a negative outlook on life. All your prophetic words will carry a tone of frustration, and even if they are correct, they do not help anyone! They do not give people hope. There is no empowerment for change here, either.

The prophetic person spends a lot of time with God, just getting cleaned up and washed by the water of the Word. So, when you see something, spend time with God asking Him about it. Listen to Him as the only one in the room, seeking to understand what it means for you. YIELD to its corrective quality in your own life.

Look to understand what you hear as if He were speaking only to you. He doesn't have an audience in mind for you. He is speaking to *you*. Receive His counsel as a personal prophetic word, even if you think it is for the church, the pastor, or your neighbour. Hear and pray through it as if another person gave you that word. What does it sound like? Do you feel shame or conviction? Do you feel love and a desire to love God? Does it sound like what you hear in Scripture?

Eat the scroll. Digest it for yourself. Know what I mean?

Chapter 7

Giants in the Land

...casting down arguments and every high thing
that exalts itself against the knowledge of God,
bringing every thought into captivity
to the obedience of Christ
(2 Corinthians 10:5)

Do you sometimes hear yourself saying things you had no knowledge of? Perhaps you suddenly glimpse information about a future event; you have no natural reason for such knowledge, yet you suddenly find yourself speaking with authority before you have even had time to process your thoughts.

Sometimes, prophetic utterances come from His Spirit through your spirit, bypassing your mind. You might have to "chew on" what you get for a period. This often happens to me in prayer.

"Lord, let me be Your Normandy." I hear myself say it and know it is God, but I don't understand what the prayer is saying or asking.

For three days, I pray and research Normandy. It is a process, sometimes, to understand what the Spirit is saying. The Holy Spirit is God. Isaiah 11 says He is the Spirit of the LORD, of Wisdom, of Understanding, of Knowledge, of Counsel, of Might, and of the Fear of the Lord. Our spirit might receive one or two of those seven dimensions. Even then, it takes a while for our brains to catch up.

Step by step, He leads me through a download of the meaning of what I will call the Normandy intercession. I cry out for a place within me for the Spirit to have a beachhead, a place to land to invade and continuously occupy in my life. I surrender my will, just like those who gave their lives in World War II, and I will be the sacrifice to enable the liberation of others. I allow the Holy Spirit to set up His home base within me. We are only as filled by the Spirit as we allow. Giving up control to Him allows Him to move. The level of power in our lives is equivalent to the level of surrender. To understand the ways of the Lord, we can look to the experience of the Israelites. He still puts us into a wilderness like He did His people back then so we can learn to trust Him no matter our circumstances. It is there we can learn how to conquer the giants.

In the new covenant, you are the land, and fear and unbelief are the giants we are most commonly up against. The wilderness is your setup to discover whether you trust God. Trusting God is always the lesson. The test is always regarding peace: Will I lose it because of what is taking place in my life?

The devil does not know what to do with a person at peace.

Israel had to cross over the Jordan to enter the Promised Land. The Jordan represents dying to self. The ultimate giant they had to overcome was, and ours still is, fear. It was not only the size of the giants that the Israelites had to conquer. It was their perceptions of themselves as grasshoppers that had to die. Most of us think spiritual warfare happens in the atmosphere around us. I contend that it occurs in the land within us! The land, the battleground, is between our ears and in our hearts!

This fight is a job only we can do! We must make use of our will. Again, stronger is he who rules his spirit than he who wins a city. (Proverbs 16:32) Why? Because the first is more complicated. Once you manage the former, you can do the latter. The expression, 'he is his own worst enemy' is often true.

This fact causes us to know we need an intercessor to fill the gap.

This is why the Lord put it in my heart to become a Normandy. It is the place of great sacrifice where things start to turn around. To win the fight against the armies around us, we must win the battle against the giants within us. God wants to establish a Normandy, a beachhead, in us first. He must win us over, conquer us. Then, we, like David, can challenge the giant for daring to defy the God of Israel. We must question everything in us that would withstand our trust in Him. This is what it means to be a Christian: to be a warrior in my own land, the land within me. With one glance of His eyes, He has undone me, and I want with all my heart to be His alone. What are the giants in your life?

What tells you that you cannot trust God?

Kill it.

Chapter 8

Kodachrome

No discipline seems pleasant at the time,
but painful. Later on, however, it produces
a harvest of righteousness and peace for those
who have been trained by it.
(Hebrews 12:11)

I reveal my age!

Are you one of my readers who remembers that Paul Simon song? "Gives us the nice bright colors/ gives us the greens of summers/ makes you think all the world's a sunny day, oh yeah/ I got a Nikon camera/I love to take a photograph/ so momma don't take my Kodachrome away…"

I dream I am going on a mission trip. People are planning which tourist sites they will go to instead of asking God where they are to go. I walk into a meeting, march right up to the front, and deliver a confrontational warning message about obedience to God instead of just deciding what we want to do. A woman standing nearby tries to convince me that my message is not from God. She decides she will play baseball instead of doing outreach with others. She is sure that because of her success as a baseball player, God would want her to use the skills she is familiar with, which is enough spirituality for her.

I tell her that her preference to play to her strengths is not biblical. She shouts, "And THAT GIVES YOU THE RIGHT TO BE SO CRITICAL, AND CONFRONTATIONAL?"

My response is, "It only takes being a little bit off plumb in the foundation to cause the building to fall. It is inevitable."

When we arrive at our destination, we all go sightseeing. The terrain is unique. Dark and indistinguishable groupings of plants are interspersed with bits of desert. As I take pictures I realize the plants are rocks. I move around changing the angles of my shots in order to get more light in the frame so that these rocks can be exposed as simulations of plants.

A man starts mocking me. He says I have become a tourist instead of a minister, just like everyone else in my group. I try to explain that bringing light to the terrain to reveal the true nature of the "plants" is the work of the gift of discernment.

That is an analogy of one aspect of the prophetic—the ability to name and discern the real from the fake. To have spiritual light and sight; to expose the difference between flesh and Spirit.

Nowadays, most of us do not use negatives in developing pictures. We do not use negative feedback we get from others, either. It is out of fashion to give an opposing opinion.

God is not a "love bunny" in the sky. But considering the prolific outpouring of positive prophetic material in Christian culture, one would think so. We, the rank and file that is, are not allowed to give any prophetic word that could be construed as negative because it points out sin.

1 Corinthians 14:3 tells us that all prophecies are given for comfort, encouragement, and edification. This passage is used to nullify words of direction or correction. It is taught in many charismatic circles that only people with prophetic office who are "capital P" prophets are allowed to correct or direct the

people of God. This is not scriptural.

So many times I have been told that it is easy to see sin in people's lives, but that it takes the Holy Spirit to call out the gold. This sounds logical and even holy, but it is not scriptural. We are called to be accountable to one another. Proverbs 27:6 says the wounds of a friend are more trustworthy than flattery.

It is time for prophetic people to proclaim the whole picture, including the negative. The body of Christ needs meat for the days ahead. Doughnuts and sugar might make us feel good, but they don't make us strong. The church is living on a diet of sweet nothings.

We swung the pendulum from only judgemental prophetic words to only allowing the "lovey-dovey" ones. People want to feel good about themselves, and the church has decided that filling that need is the only purpose of the prophetic. We make our people feel happy, believing in a non-demanding "moralistic therapeutic deism"[1] instead of coming face to face with the God of the Bible. But we need words of correction that point us back to righteous living.

The use of negatives is part of the process of photography. Willingness to consider what might be construed as negative words and to ask the Lord if they are true and taking it to scripture is part of the process of developing our character.

---

1   This is a term coined by sociologists Christian Smith and Melina Lundquist Denton in their book *Soul Searching: The Religious and Spiritual Lives of American Teenagers* (Oxford University Press).

Chapter 9

Where Have all the Fathers Gone?

"For the Lord disciplines those he loves
and he punishes each one he accepts as his child."
As you endure this divine discipline,
remember that God is treating you
as his own children.
Who ever heard of a child who was never
disciplined by his father?
(Hebrews 12:6, NLT)

I dream there is a noisy chaotic house full of children. Three social workers are sitting in various places observing and taking notes. They make recommendations and proposals of care, but the children run their own house. The older children boss, the younger ones around, but no one listens, it's all about playtime. As I walk through the home, I am struck that there is no bathroom. There will be no rules about baths or brushing of teeth.

My chest feels heavy and painful when I first wake up. I pray, and I feel a sense of grief. Suddenly, I am overcome with the burden of intercession. I do not know how to explain it, but I know that the house in my dream stands for the Church. It consists of children telling each other what to do and professional staff who do not intervene and bring order. (There are also not enough staff for the number of children, but that is a side point.)

The church has staff, but they do not live there. They are hired and work office hours, in essence separate from what is going on. They do not have the responsibility of parents. What comes to mind is I Corinthians 4:14-17, Paul's injunction:

I do not write these things to shame you but to admonish you as my beloved children. If you were to have countless teachers in Christ, you would not have many fathers, for in Christ Jesus, I became your Father through the gospel. Therefore, I exhort you to be imitators of me. For this reason, I have sent Timothy to you, my beloved and faithful child in the Lord, and he will remind you of my ways, which are in Christ, just as I teach everywhere in every Church.

Many of us want the authority to dictate others' behavior. Some even have a well-meaning desire to care for the troublemakers. But only a few of us are willing to live in the sacrificial and committed ways of our parents. The day-in and day-out drudgery of life is where we often find it necessary to put ourselves last on our list of priorities. Social workers are often helpful and skilled, and they do important work. But they do not replace parents. They do not replace family. If the Church were to believe and behave like family, I am sure the "house" would look vastly different from the one in my dream.

The absence of a bathroom was notable in this house of undisciplined siblings and no parents. The bathroom represents releasing what is toxic; from a spiritual standpoint this consists of confession and repentance.

Why was it significant that no place was given for confession or repentance in the house? Siblings living together in a house will have little interest in child-raising responsibilities compared to their parents. Children can boss each other around, and may even enjoy doing so, but they don't have the time, patience, or incentive to care about the often-difficult task of correction. They are not invested in seeing repentance and change in behavior.

I hear the song:

Where have all the flowers (fathers) gone?
Long time passing.
Where have all the fathers gone?
A long time ago...

Chapter 10

The Promise Keeper

I will betroth you to Me forever;
I will betroth you to Me
in righteousness and in justice,
in steadfast love and in mercy.
I will betroth you to me in faithfulness,
and you shall know the Lord.
(Hosea 2:19-20)

If we are faithless, He remains faithful;
for He cannot disown Himself.
(2 Timothy 2:13)

*T*he *presence* of the Holy Spirit hovers over me in the early morning hours as I sit quietly, waiting. Peace saturates my mind and emotions and even the air around me. His whisper comes, "I am the First and Original 'Promise Keeper.'"

With all the good intentions of the man who started the Promise Keeper movement, we still find that all men are unfaithful.

Romans 3:3-4 True, some of them were unfaithful, but just because they were unfaithful, does that mean God will be unfaithful. Let God be true and every man
a liar.

I would be remiss if I did not include a chapter about how God changed my heart and put a new spirit in me about His promise and covenant with Israel. I wish I could write an entire book about that subject—God's unending love for Israel, His beloved..

Here is an encounter I experienced: I am in church. My heart is full of worship, and I am engulfed with the Lord's presence. A sense of timelessness and weightlessness overtakes me. My consciousness is filled with awe, and the experience of God's love overwhelms me. It keeps building to a crescendo.

I cannot take it and burst into tears. A dam breaks, and I cannot restrain myself. I weep and shake as God fills me with love.

And this love has a focus. I understand that this love is His heart for His firstborn, Israel. A melody fills my ears and lyrics come:

> You are the one.
> You are still the one I want. You are still the one.
> I have not rejected you. You are the one, you are still the one I choose; you are still the one.
> How I long to gather you, you are still the one.
> You are the one I long for, you are the one.
> You are the one I long for, you are the one.

Like many of the encounters I have with God, this one is no different. It is a marker on my spiritual timeline. Life is brought down to a before and after the experience. Things were one way; this happened, and everything after it was different.

Proof of an encounter is the fruit. Since that encounter, I consistently pray for Israel. I discovered many wonderful ministries who facilitate providing Zoom platforms for those whose hearts are dedicated to "pray for the Peace of Jerusalem" and the call to "Comfort ye, My people." These are fantastic people with whom I have developed deep friendships and partnerships in prayer, and this is a major part of what God is doing in my life. He has changed me dramatically.

The Lord has not changed His mind about his covenant with the state of Israel. It is a lie from the pit of hell that God has replaced the Jewish nation with His bride, the church, Christianity. Jesus and the apostles who authored the New Testament did not intend to start a new religion. On the contrary, God expanded the promises of the covenant with Israel and God opened the door for Gentiles to enter the covenant He started with the Jews.

Satan has fooled us by replacement theology and robbed us. Israel was not permanently erased to make room for the church.

We may acknowledge that Christianity has Jewish roots, but some of us have divorced ourselves from the Jewish family. It is like a bride who agrees to marry but refuses to meet her bridegroom's parents. We have treated the roots of our faith like a sperm bank, instead of a family that is so rich with the knowledge and covenants of God. Just give us our Messiah.

We do not care to know what happened in the past. We are starting a new family with new rules and traditions. We have bitten off our nose to spite our face. It is the God of Abraham and Isaac and Jacob who is the Father and Lord of us all. We did not start a new religion, we became a part of the "household of God"; Israel is our older brother. God did not plant a new tree in his garden; he grafted us into the ancient root of covenant.

Companies and apps that allow us to explore our DNA ancestry proliferate in our society. We can find answers to the question of our identity there. What about our spiritual DNA and ancestry? We can only find our identity and destiny when we recognize and accept our place in a much bigger picture. A picture that includes the God of the Old Testament, the God of the Jews. We cry out for purpose and fulfillment as individuals. God wants to answer. He wants to remove the walls in our mind that have shut out the current people and geography of the state of Israel.

We come to know our purpose only when we come to know Him, Jesus, King of the Jews. He is still the promise keeper.

Isaiah 54:10 For the mountains may move and the hills disappear, but even then, my faithful love for you will remain. My covenant of blessing will never be broken," says the Lord, who has compassion on you.

Chapter 11

Mirror, Mirror

And Jesus said to them,
"And who do you say that I am?"
(Matthew 16:15)

What do you see when you look in the mirror?

1 Corinthians 13:12 For now we see in a mirror dimly, but then face to face; now I know in part, but then I will know fully just as I have been fully known.

2 Corinthians 3:18 We can all draw close to him with the veil removed from our faces. And with no veil, we all become like mirrors that brightly reflect the glory of the Lord Jesus. We are being transfigured into his very image as we move from one brighter level of glory to another. This glorious transfiguration comes from the Lord, who is the Spirit.

1 John 3:2-3 Beloved, now we are children of God, and it has not appeared yet what we will be. We know that when He appears, we will be like Him because we will see Him just as He is. And everyone who has this hope fixed on Him purifies himself, just as He is pure.

The woman I used to see in the mirror struggled with low self-esteem from early childhood. Neglect and abuse distorted the image I saw in the mirror. I experienced a profound transformation when I was introduced to the love of God in Jesus. I read the Bible, then experienced what I read about by the power of His Holy Spirit.

*Romans 5:5 and hope does not disappoint because
the love of God has been poured out within our hearts
through the Holy Spirit who was given to us.*

Now, I quietly read Scripture and just think about God. My eyes are often closed, but suddenly, I can see Him very clearly. He is shining and surrounded by light, and when He looks at me, His eyes sparkle with joy. I can tell He likes what He sees! As I gaze at Him, I see myself the way He sees me. Some of my good qualities appear magnified, and I hear Him say, "I see Me in you." Any sense of self-consciousness or condemnation is absent, and I am free just to BE. As I look at Him, seeing who He is, it is like He becomes a mirror. I can see what He sees. I catch a glimpse of the person that I will be for eternity, and am aware there is no more shame, no sorrow, no sin.

Love, grace, dignity, and generosity clothe and surround me. Everything I thought I lacked I find I have in the Lord. All the foolishness and wickedness the enemy accuses me of is GONE. God is eternal, therefore outside of and unbound by time. He sees right now the person we will be in eternity—the person we are being transformed into, from glory to glory, as it says in 2 Corinthians 3:18

There is a common goal-setting trend known as "vision boards." People collate an assortment of pictures and objects that call to mind the goals of the future: Where might they be in five or ten years?

What if you could envision the person you would be in heaven? The person who is completely accepted and loved with all of the negative effects of being born in sin GONE. The person who is ONLY GOOD. Untwisted my selfishness or bitterness, fear or insecurity? How might that change or motivate you? Have you seen a glimpse of yourself that way? Who is the you that you will be for eternity?

If not, ask God to show you. He sees the you that you will be in the millennium.

I am not talking about being preoccupied with yourself;we know that we will be like Him when we see Him as He is. We purify ourselves with this hope.

Growing in God is about becoming who we actually ARE in Him.

Spend time looking at HIM by reading the Bible and in times of worship and prayer.

Strive for that upward call in Christ Jesus (Philippians 3:14). And let everything else fall away.

Chapter 12

A Sunday Buffet

Why should any living mortal or any man
offer complaint in view of his sins? Let us
examine and prove our ways,
and let us return to the Lord.
(Lamentations 3:39-40)

Who does not like a buffet? Something about the "all you can eat" concept is appealing. Tables loaded with multiple varieties of foods all in one place. I love tasting food from different cuisines that I have never learned to cook or that are made with ingredients too expensive for my food budget.

I dream I am at a luxurious buffet. I go up to the table three times, and each time I meet the same woman with her face twisted into a sour look. Along with her expression, she has critical words for every single food she tries. I warn her each time I approach that I will tell her to leave if she can find nothing to please her. Why is she staying if only to grumble?

But at each course, she declares that nothing is acceptable to her.

As I wake up, I hear "the table of the Lord and the table of demons." We find this phrase in 1 Corinthians 10:21: You cannot drink the cup of the Lord and the cup of demons; you cannot partake of the table of the Lord and the table of demons."

This is an exciting chapter of Corinthians, and I hope you can take the time to read it. Four subjects are addressed: temptations, complaining, communion, and idol feasts.

These verses in 1 Corinthians remind us that the truths of the New Testament are rooted in the Old.

There we find baptism (into the cloud and sea), communion (manna and water from the rock), healing (raising of the snake on the pole), and...complaining and idolatry.

Wow; why are these grouped together? I suggest they are all connected to the same message. We are one in Christ, and what one member does affects the entire body. Paul was lumping together complaining and idolatry because they are sins of the same ilk and equally important.

What if the buffet in my dream symbolizes the Lord's table, and the woman finds fault in what God has given her in life? Today, we tend to think complaining is a minor sin. But look at how God was forced to deal with Israel because of their continual complaints.

In the dream, I tell the woman who complains that she must go and cannot partake in the buffet if she is only going to complain.

Identify wherever these kind of ssues live in your heart and cut them off. What does the table of the Lord have to do with the table of demons? What does fellowship with God and the sense of His Presence have to do with partaking in complaining? Again, can we remind ourselves of just where that behaviour led the Israelites? The Lord has mercy and forgives us, but we are also expected to gain experience in grace, which means leaving behind old attitudes.

Just like in my dream, we must tell complaining that it must go. Call it for what it is, and exert the same energy you would if you were to discover any other door open to the occult.

I think of a time when God did not seem to mind someone complaining.

> *Exodus 11:11 So Moses asked the LORD, "Why have You been so hard on Your servant? And why have I not found favor in Your sight, that You have laid the burden of all these people on me? Was it I who conceived all these people? Was it I who brought them forth that You should say to me, 'Carry them in your bosom as a nurse carries a nursing infant to the land which You swore to their fathers'? Where am I to get meat to give to all these people? They weep before me, saying, 'Give us meat that we may eat!' I alone cannot carry all these people because it is too burdensome. So if You are going to deal thus with me, please kill me at once, if I have found favor in Your sight, and do not let me see my wretchedness."*

Moses was complaining to God about the job He had given him, and God's response was not anger. He did not get angry or give Moses a lecture. He answered with mercy and introduced what I see as one of the first instances of delegating tasks when a leader is burned out.

Look at the beginning of the same chapter. In verse 1 it tells us that God was angered by complaints:

Now the people became like those who complain of adversity in the hearing of the Lord; and when the Lord heard it, His anger was kindled, and the fire of the Lord burned among them and consumed the outskirts of the camp.

What was the difference? I suggest that there is a difference between complaining to the Lord and against the Lord.

*Numbers 21:7 And the people came to Moses and said, "We have sinned, for we have spoken against the L*ORD *and against you. Pray to the L*ORD *that he takes away the serpents from us." So, Moses prayed for the people.*

The difference? Heart attitude. Moses had seen and believed in the goodness of God, and pouring out His heart to God because He TRUSTED that goodness. The Israelites complaints were an accusation against God's heart.

There are at least fifty-seven Bible verses about complaining. Moses, Jonah, Job, David, and the Israelites (most often) complained at some point.

The complaints in our hearts against God are an open door for demonic entities to have footholds or "rights" in our lives that produce further consequences.

To complain: verb to express dissatisfaction or annoyance about a situation or an event, protest, grumble, make a fuss, object, criticize, find fault, kick up a fuss, or raise a stink.

In Numbers 12, God asks Miriam and Aaron why they were not afraid to complain against Moses, and there were disastrous results.

The grace of the New Testament does not change the fact that there are consequences to our actions.

We need to do two things: come to the table of the Lord and ask forgiveness.

Then, we need to stop complaining against God.

Chapter 13

Drive Through Devotions

Then the Lord would speak to Moses face to face as one speaks to a friend. Then Moses would return to the camp, but his young aide Joshua son of Nun did not leave the tent.
(Exodus 33:11)

You know the feeling!

You are sitting in your favorite chair, the devoted chair, the dedicated time, the right music, and the daily reading accomplished.

I have done well. I sit waiting for my reward, my treat. I HEAR. Yes, hearing is my reward! And I relish every word. If the Lord is speaking with me, that is proof that He is satisfied with me, or that I have pleased Him in some way.

I write and record, self-satisfied. Another "quiet time" under my belt. I have in my hot little hand what I came to receive. My fresh word. My daily bread. Now, I can believe that I am okay with God! He still talks to me; I must be on His good side. Pride reaches around and pats my shoulder, "Well done."

"UH-oh." There is tension in the air. I can sense I am about to be corrected. The expression "air so thick you could cut it with a knife" comes to mind.

The razor sharp voice slices, "Is that all you wanted?" the Lord asks. I pause; my heart is beating a little faster.

"What is that, Lord?

"Did you get what you came for? Do you want fries with that?"

My heart sinks down into my stomach; conviction grows and flares until it reaches my cheeks in a blush of shame. The voice of the Lord asks again, "Is that all you wanted? Your word for the day, and now you are going to leave?"

In that "you could hear a pin drop" silence, His sharp rebuke stings.

"Is it all you want, and that is enough for you? 'Feed me so I can feel good about myself!' I can go with my trophy, my 'word for the day,' to share with others and be known as a prophet. I might as well ask if you want fries with that. Would a word from anyone do? You just want to look for my hand to feed you, or you stay until you can hear My words and see My Face. I supply the birds of the air from My hand. I can make a donkey speak. Is there any place for pride in this scenario? I have created you as one able to spend time with Me, for My own sake, to get to know Me, to be in a relationship with Me, not so you can hear My words and use them for your own benefit."

Realization dawns, I can actually grieve God even in my "pursuit of Him." Using someone as a means to an end is not something we recommend among friends—and He is God! He is not a thing, He is a person, and that is hurtful.

I respond to His rebuke by settling more deeply into my chair. I will not move. I will stay with Him until He stops talking. And long after. I have learned this lesson. My time with Him is not just about ticking a job off a good Christian list. He showed me quite clearly that this was a two-way conversation that was not about getting my needs met, but getting to know Him. What is on His mind?

I do not rush away, but wait until I sense the peace that comes after finishing a conversation with a friend and knowing it is time to go on with the day. My friend and I have both shared our hearts and there is natural resolve between us.

And when I meet with the Lord, we are not simply friends. As I already noted, He is God! So, He is worthy of more respect than my cursory acknowledgement.

How do you spend your time with God?

Chapter 14

The Power of the Blood

For the message of the cross is foolishness to those who are perishing, but to us who are being saved it is the power of God. For it is written "I will destroy the wisdom of the wise and bring to nothing the understanding of the prudent." Where is the wise? Where is the scribe? Where is the debater of this age? Has not God made foolish the wisdom of this world? For since in the wisdom of God, the world through wisdom did not know God, it pleased God through the foolishness of the message preached to save those who believe. (1 Corinthians 1:18-21)

Let me begin with 1 Corinthians 1:26-31:

For consider your calling, brethren, that there were not many wise according to the flesh, not many mighty, not many noble; but God has chosen the foolish things of the world to shame the wise, and God has chosen the weak things of the world to shame the things that are strong, and the base things of the world and the despised God has chosen, the things that are not, so that He may nullify the things that are, so that no man may boast before God. But by His doing you are in Christ Jesus, who became to us wisdom from God, righteousness, sanctification, and redemption, so that, just as it is written, "Let him who boasts, boast in the Lord."

I attended a very traditional Baptist church at the beginning of my journey into the things of the Holy Spirit.

One particular Sunday, as I am worshipping, the Holy Spirit falls on me and I enter an encounter. I have a vision of myself covered in the blood of Jesus. I am enveloped in an intense sense of peace as I look at this vision of being covered by blood.

In the peace and stillness, I hear the Lord whisper, "The blood of Jesus is slippery, and in every place the blood is, the demons that have bothered you no longer have a hold; neither will they ever be able to grab on wherever my blood is."

I see a horde of demons flying out of me, and I hear their screams. I wonder where they will go and think of when Jesus sent the legion of demons into the pigs (Matthew 8:38-34).

I am incredulous; I can hardly believe what is happening; I can only let go and yield. Then warm, soothing oil starts pouring over my head. Love and peace go as deeply as the pain and torment had been. I am in my own bubble, completely unaware of where I am or what is happening to my body. I am shaking violently, but I don't feel it. No one knows what is going on with me.

A sizable percentage of the congregation does not believe in the gifts and ministry of the Holy Spirit—never mind the existence of demons or the ministry of deliverance. Does that bother God? HA! Not in the slightest! Yes there I was in that conservative Baptist church, the pastor calling upon me to stand up and tell the congregation what is happening to me? And my response? Why, Jesus said to me that the blood of Jesus is slippery! Because it is slippery, no demon can hang on to me! How is that for theological reasoning for the complainants saying demons do not exist, and if they did, they could not bother Christians?

God takes great delight in baffling the world's wisdom by using the simplicity of preaching the story of the cross. Consider your calling that not many of you could be called wise theologians! God has chosen the foolish things to shame the wise. The blood of Jesus is slippery! It is a simple yet profound depiction of a truth that a child could understand. We, indeed, can be free of any influence of the demonic by reminding ourselves that Jesus already died to nullify their power.

You must become like little children to enter the kingdom.

Chapter 15

The Whisper

So husbands ought to love their own wives
as their own bodies; he who loves his wife
loves himself. For no one ever hated his own flesh,
but nourishes and cherishes it
just as the Lord does the church.
(Ephesians 5:28)

1 Kings 19:11 So He said, "Go forth and stand on the mountain before the Lord. And behold, the Lord was passing by! And a great and strong wind was rending the mountains and breaking in pieces the rocks before the Lord, but the Lord was not in the wind. After that, an earthquake, but the Lord was not in the earthquake. After the earthquake, a fire, but the Lord was not in the fire, and after the fire, the gentle whisper. When Elijah heard it, he wrapped his face in his mantle and went out and stood at the entrance of the cave. And behold, a voice came to him and said, "What are you doing, Elijah?

This morning, I hear the Lord whisper, "I am fond of man, and I am fond of you." Along with the words comes the now familiar sense of cool clear water rising up my body. I am being washed and feel so accepted and renewed. Like a little child being bathed by my father.

It was then He also whispered "Benevolence". Such a simple word! But it had an incredible sense of love. The Lord's tone of voice has such tenderness and depth. It is almost a unique viscosity. It is thick,

It is like a combination of oil, aloe and molasses. Perhaps that is how to describe a healing balm.

I decided to look up the word "fond."

The dictionary definition of "fond" of someone is to have affection for, love, tenderness towards, cherish, and lavish affection. To prize highly. To be told someone is fond of you is to know that when they think of you, they smile and have a warm feeling in their heart.

Coincidentally, I read twice about affection in the Scripture this morning.

Philippians 1:8 -10 For God is my witness, how I long for you all with the affection of Christ Jesus. And this I pray, that your love may overflow still more and more in real knowledge and all discernment, so that you may discover the things that are excellent, that you may be sincere and blameless for the day of Christ.

Philippians 2:1-2 Therefore, if there is any encouragement in Christ, if any consolation of love, if any fellowship of the Spirit, if any affection and compassion, make my joy complete by being of the same mind, maintaining the same love, united in Spirit, intent on one purpose.

The word for "affection" in this verse describes a longing for, or to be affectionately desirous.

The Whisper

Deuteronomy 10:15 Yet the Lord set His affections on your fathers and chose their descendants after them, even you, above all peoples, as it is this day.

The word translated affection in this verse is from the Hebrew meaning "to love long and with delight."

2 Corinthians 7:15 His affection abounds all the more toward you as he remembers your obedience, How you received him with fear and trembling.

This word translated from the Greek as affection refers to "tender mercy from the inward parts of the spleen."

Can you apply all these words to what you believe God's attitude toward you is? He longs for you and delights in you. He has tender mercy for you. He cherishes you; he prizes you highly.

He wants to dote on you. He thinks of you often.

Psalm 139:17-18 How precious also are Your thoughts for me, God! How vast is the sum of them! Were I to count them, they would outnumber the sand. When I awake, I am still with You.

The revelation that I had this morning of His fondness for us is like a sliver of a dark mirror of what is possible to understand, the truth of His thoughts toward us, which are incomprehensible.

Receive His love!

Chapter 16

Like the Dew

May my teaching drop like the rain,
my speech condense like the dew,
like gentle rain on grass,
like showers on new growth.
(Deuteronomy 32:2)

Have you ever walked barefoot on the dew-soaked grass in the early morning? We learned in grade six science how the dew was created, but there is nothing like walking barefoot in it to experience the wonder of it.

There is a way the Lord speaks that feels just like this. The Holy Spirit settles imperceptibly, and so quietly. It feels as if He is coming both from inside and upon me at the same time. I become hyper-focused, concentrating intently upon His presence even while feeling completely relaxed. Then, the word is just "there." He speaks, and I know what He has said without trying to perceive it. Even though I very much enjoy this deep sweet and subtle way that I hear Him, I often wish I heard Him in ways that I hear others share His voice.

Like, with fire and thunder and crackles of electricity. I hear that way occasionally, but most often it is as I have described to you. His word quietly drifts and settles like the dew. Is this quiet distillation of the spirit the primary way you hear from God? Have you wished you heard from God differently than the way you do?

The Word says the voice of the Lord is the sound of many waters. I don't believe this simply means that His voice is like a waterfall. His voice is as the sound of many KINDS of waters. There can be the super-charged electric words from God that sound like mighty waters breaking through a dam. He also leads us beside the STILL waters in Psalm 23 which intimates the kind of peace His voice can impart. The Lord refers to Himself as a spring of living water in Jeremiah 2:13 A spring describes water that is bubbling. Sometimes the voice of the Lord bubbles up in us of its own accord and it is only after we hear ourselves say the words that we realize that it was the Lord speaking, that He momentarily took over our speech.

Isaiah 35:7 says that the Lord makes parched ground into pools. What a difference! The place of lack of want, changed into a pool a place of satisfaction, refreshment, even a place where one can return to for supply! The brook, a small stream, the place where Elijah was made to rest and to be fed by the ravens. This speaks to me of something we find on our own on a solitary hike. Its for our own personal use.

Let us listen for the various kinds of waters of the voice of God. Here is the spring, the brook, the pool, the waterfall, and the sea.

The Lord speaks in countless ways; let us listen to them all!

Let's ask Him to let us Hear Him in the infinite number of ways He speaks!

Let us walk barefoot in the grass; covered in dew, let us wait for His word!

Chapter 17

I Choose You

For now have I chosen
and sanctified this house,
that My name may be there forever;
and My eyes and My heart
shall be there perpetually.
(2 Chronicles 7:16)

It is a summer evening, the heat yet to wane. Soaking like a cat in in my easy chair the haze gave way to a dreamy atmosphere and I drifted off to another place. I am on a hilltop of resplendent green. The smell of hot grass and wildflowers drift in on the slightest of breezes and I see him.

The most beautiful Man is making His way toward me, of all people! My breath catches in my throat as He bends down on one knee. With His arms extended toward me, He takes my hands in His, looks in my eyes with tenderness and softly says," I choose YOU for my bride. Say yes?"

Jesus asks me to choose HIM! I am overwhelmed; my body trembles, my senses flooded with love, surprise, delight as I take in this moment. He is here, with me, asking for my hand!

Wanting me! The feeling of intimacy between us is palpable.

We toss the phrase "bride of Christ" about so carelessly that its substance and significance drains. It ceases to affect us personally. That we are part of His bride should invoke an emotional response in our hearts.

Look at Ephesians 5. Most sermons use verses 22-33 to teach how husbands and wives are to behave toward one another. Yet it is so much more! Verse 32 says plainly: "This mystery is great, but I am speaking with reference to Christ and the church." The mystery of marriage demonstrates Jesus's heart attitude toward us, His bride!

*Ephesians 5:28-29 So husbands ought also to love their wives as their own bodies. He who loves his own wife loves himself; for no one ever hated his own flesh, but nourishes and cherishes it, **just as Christ also does the church.***

Jesus's heart's desire is to nourish and cherish His bride. Do you know this about yourself?

Do you walk in this knowledge experientially, knowing that His heart is so for you, so tender toward you?

Meditate on the meanings of these words. To nourish is to feed, maintain, nurse, nurture, and supply with food and support.

To cherish is to have a great affection for, prize, cling to, hold dear, treasure, care for, love, pamper, and shelter. Do you know God has thoughts like these toward you?

Jesus chose you to be part of His bride in the garden of Gethsemane. His desire for you, His Bride is more significant than regard for His own life.

The commitment between a husband and wife is a dim reflection of His love for us. Earthly marriages fail, but His covenant with us will never fail. He does not take His commitment lightly. He will not fall out of love or hit the road when the going gets tough.

When a woman receives a proposal, she has a choice: she can say no. It is not one-sided affair. The man has chosen her, but will she also choose him? Above all others?

What does it mean to say yes to becoming his bride? A woman says yes to becoming engaged, which happens once. The marriage itself is a continual reiteration of that "yes."

When we say yes to the Lord, we believe in and receive His love and act in ways that reflect that love.

A woman who is proposed to often has a glow that results from being chosen. As such, she is secure in the knowledge she is favored, hand-picked, selected, and first choice.

Look up the antonym of chosen to discover the lies the enemy tells us!

The voice of the deceiver tells us that we are not special, we are ordinary, run-of-the-mill, average.

SAY YES!

Walk in the identity you have been given as the bride of Christ, Creator of the universe!

Take His proffered hand and walk in a manner worthy of your calling!

Be nourished and cherished by Him, your Husband, and feed His love to others.

I am compelled to tell you. I feel like a bride on the first morning of her honeymoon, who rejoices that she had just had the most beautiful night and celebration with her beloved. She can hardly take in her good fortune that she GETS to spend every day with him from now on for the rest of her life. It is just beginning!

She hugs this knowledge to herself, and joy overflows as she looks out the window on her new life.

As the bride of Christ, intimacy with Him is our primary responsibility as His wife.

No caveats.

Chapter 18

So Come

That which was from the beginning, which we have heard, which we have seen with our eyes, which we have looked upon, and our hands have handled, concerning the Word of life— —the life was manifested, and we have seen, and bear witness, and declare to you that eternal life which was with the Father and was manifested to us— that which we have seen and heard we declare to you, that you may also have fellowship with us; and truly our fellowship is with the Father and with His Son Jesus Christ.
(1 John 1:1-4)

I come to meet with the Lord. We spend time together with no agenda. I begin to sense His heart, and mine begins to hurt and ache. The sensation increases, and I go to my knees. I feel sorrow, His sorrow. It becomes a heavy spiritual burden. My stomach starts to hurt, and I feel a burning within, as if on fire. The only way to alleviate the pain is to rock back and forth, my arms across my stomach.

I begin calling out in prayer for the awakening of intercessors to pick up their pails and shovels and re-dig the wells of revival in Canada. I weep for the people who have yet to feel the love of God. I weep Jesus's tears of longing for a very personal relationship with each of us. I cry until the assurance comes that He hears my prayer, receives my tears, and promises to answer. The wonderful thing about birthing something in the Spirit is that you experience a beginning, a middle, and an end. When you are pregnant, you are pregnant; it is a black-and-white situation. There WILL be a resolution somehow, even if the outcome is negative. There is something alive inside you, and something will happen to it! When travail in prayer comes, it does not lift until there is birthing. Until the breakthrough comes and you know that you know that you know that you have the answer to your prayer.

Exhausted, I fall asleep and dream. I am walking with an unidentified woman, and she takes me to a cottage that is so at one with its surroundings that you might miss it. But the door is red and inviting. The woman opens the door and leads me down a set of stairs that descend until I come to a large underground room. It is the average height of a typical apartment but it has dirt floors. I somehow know this apartment is available for rent. We walk through it, and I discover a bedroom and a kitchen with a patio door, through which I see a tranquil seating arrangement for the tenants to enjoy the outdoors together. The rooms are modestly furnished but cozy and peaceful. Continuing our tour, we find a library where an old man sits with his back to us. I somehow know he is the apartment's owner who quietly waits while we search his home. I am slightly embarrassed and feel like a trespasser. He gets up to greet us, but I run out because I'm unsure if I have been caught doing something wrong.

I wake up and contemplate this adventure in dreamland. Going about the business of starting the day, I cannot stop thinking about the cottage, its peace, and the dignified, humble owner. I wish for a different ending to the dream. Instead of running away from him, I wish I had stayed and spent time soaking up the atmosphere of that untroubled setting and getting to know the quiet yet commanding man.

It is then that I remember in my intercession the previous day I had labored in the Spirit for the re-digging of wells of revival. I know by the Spirit that the two are connected. I had been welcomed to a place to live that had been dug out by prayer. I sit down in my "quiet time" chair and wait for the Lord to show me more of the dream's meaning. I wait, and the Lord, ever faithful to me, leads me to understand the secrets of wisdom to be found in that nighttime scenario.

When I dream of an unidentified woman, she represents the Holy Spirit. She leads me deeper into the things of God, which are accessed through a downward trek to humility. There are rooms yet to be discovered in the realm of the Spirit. The Father has opened these rooms for us and is waiting for us to investigate and, more importantly, to sit down with Him. He has seated us in heavenly places. Ephesians 2:6: The way up is first going down through the cross.

John 14:1-2: "Do not worry or surrender to your fear. For you have believed in God, now trust and believe in me also. My Father's house has many dwelling places. If it were, otherwise, I would tell you plainly because I go to prepare a place for you to rest."

Now, we know this scripture refers to places in heaven. Yet there are places available to us to experience Him in the heavenly realm while we live on earth!

Why did I run out at the end of the dream? This is what we do sometimes when we experience the Holy Spirit. We go in, but we come out quickly. We enter an encounter with God, but we do not linger; we want to be back in our comfort zone. The air of the supernatural is different than the realm of the natural world, and we need to acclimate ourselves to it because most of us don't want to stay long. We are more accustomed to being in the natural realm, in our "body suits." It is like astronauts in training who practice in anti-gravity suits. We need to practice sitting under the weight of God's presence, not moving until He does.

God is inviting us to LIVE in these new rooms, not just to visit! But they will cost us something! The currency we use is faith and obedience and humility. As we exercise it, we can live more consistently in the power and presence of the Holy Spirit. In these wonderful places He has prepared for us to inhabit in His gentle, intimate but commanding Presence.

Chapter 19

Resting Place

Jesus said to him, "You shall love
the Lord your God with all your heart
and with all your soul
and with all your mind."
(Matthew 22: 37)

I am listening to an old Vineyard song by Brian Doerksen, "Resting Place." While I am resting in this song I see in the middle of a room a woman washing the floor. A circle of light floods the area where she is cleaning, but outside the circle, it is dark, and she cannot reach those sections on her hands and knees. Scattered around the room's dark corners, I realized there is clutter that has not been exposed.

I sense the Lord ask, "Is this how you would prepare your place if you were expecting a visit from royalty? Would you want a visiting monarch to have to step over things and stay only within the confines of that circle of the floor you allowed the light to shine, restricted to the part you have cleaned?

"Would you not prepare for them a place to sit and REST? Would you not clean right into the corners? I want to fill you entirely with My Presence, and to do that, you must allow me into the places where My light has yet to shine."

Imagine a spiritual life like a physical room, only cleaned in the middle and not in the corners.

The Lord is light, and no impurity can be found in Him.

> *1 John 1:5 "This is the message we have heard from him and declare to you: God is light; in him, there is no darkness."*

The Lord makes clean the place where He rests. We must also permit Him to go to places we have not visited. We all have hidden things in the dark we have not wanted exposed to the light. He wants to bring so much more light to our lives!

The displayed, exhibited, and demonstrated Presence of God requires more than a partial offering from us.

Love so amazing and divine demands my soul, my life, my all.

Chapter 20

Stay

You will show me the path of life;
In your presence is fullness of joy;
at your right hand are pleasures for evermore
(Psalm 16:11)

"*Stay with me.*"

There are so many love songs with this pining sentiment expressed.

We are created in God's image, and He loves us like that. I want you to hear it.

Hear His desire for you: "Stay with me."

The book of Ruth is a well-known story in the Bible. The title character, newly widowed after her father-in-law and husband have died, speaks a famous line to her mother-in-law, Naomi.

> *"Do not urge me to leave you or turn back from following you, for where you go, I will go, and where you stay, I will stay. Your people shall be my people, and your God, my God." Ruth 1:16.*

Let me weave that with another story of a similar theme: a man tells his older mentor that he will not let him out of sight. In the story of Elijah and Elisha, Elijah seems to WANT to dismiss his pupil for him to go away.

> *Elijah said to Elisha, "Stay here. please, for the L*ORD *has sent me as far as Bethel." But Elisha said, "As the L*ORD *lives and as you live, I will not leave you."*
> 2 *Kings* 2:2

Three times, Elijah tests Elisha, and each time, just as Ruth did, Elisha responds that he will NOT leave Elijah's side. I use the word "test" because that is what it was.

Elisha had to be willing to go further in his journey of "staying" to receive his "mantle."

This brings another story to my mind. In John 6 Jesus fed the multitude with two loaves and five fish that were given to Him. He perceived that many wanted to make him king because of this miraculous sign so He departed. He later went on to explain that they should follow Him not just so they could have their physical needs looked after. That He was the true bread from heaven, they must also eat the flesh and drink the blood if they wanted to have true life. This was a difficult thing to accept and many were offended and stopped following Him.

Jesus turns to His disciples and says, "Will you leave also?" I can almost see His piercing gaze and almost hear his tender heart question, "will you stay with me?"

Simon Peter gives that famous reply in verse 68:

Simon Peter answered, "Lord, to whom shall we go? You have words of eternal life."

I believe each of these stories is a picture of the kind of relationship God desires to have with us.

He seeks those who refuses to go away or be sent out, to walk away, or to be offended. Those who see and know the power of life that rests within our relationship with Him.

A vast number of love songs express the desire of the human heart to find a loved one.

Someone who wants to STAY.

STAY with me. Be devoted only to me.

We were created in the Lord's image. Hear His desire for you.

Matthew 26:38-40 Then He said to them, "My soul is deeply grieved, to the point of death; STAY here and keep watch with Me." And He went a little beyond them, fell on His face, and prayed, saying, "My Father, if it is possible, let this cup pass from Me; yet not as I will, but as You will." And He came to the disciples and found them sleeping, and He said to Peter, "So, you men could not STAY and watch with Me for one hour?"

Know this. Your hunger for a relationship is not because you desire a romantic partner.

You have this hunger because God made you to be like HIM.

HE wants a relationship with YOU. Open your heart!

Chapter 21

Intimate

"Oh my dove, in the clefts of the rock,
in the secret places of the stairs,
let me see your face,
let me hear your voice;
for sweet is your voice,
and your face is lovely."
(Song of Solomon 2:14)

Song of Solomon 4: 9 "You have captured my heart, my sister, my bride. With a single strand of your necklace made my heartbeat faster with a single glance of your eyes."

*T*he poem's subject, the Shulamite woman of Solomon's song, did not need to do anything to capture his attention. She HAD already captured his heart; he spoke in the past tense. So, it is with us, God's creation: we already HAVE His attention. We are His pearl of great price. He already gave everything for us.

Matthew 13:45: "Again, the kingdom of heaven is like a merchant seeking fine pearls, and upon finding one pearl of immense value, he sold all he had and bought it."

I have heard many people preach that we must sell all to buy the kingdom. This is true. But it is also true that God purchased us first. We were *His* pearl of great price.

In a dream, I meet up with a man I know has come to teach me something. I know him. and his tone of voice. He is masculine and his tone is instructive and kind. He tells me I am being given a secret reward that no one else would be allowed to see.

He gives me a suitcase which I open as he stands by looking. Inside I find a brassiere adorned with diamonds and pearls. It is carefully arranged on black velvet fabric like that used to display diamonds.

On awakening, I feel a heat in my cheeks and a warmth inside me. I know the instructor is Jesus and he is choosing me as His bride. I am flushed with delight and can hardly believe He wants me! He wants to see me as no one else sees me.

If this was to be a secret and the gift so private, why do I share it with you? The intimate garment stands for something He wants for all of us.

> *Psalm 45:10-14 Listen, O daughter, give attention and incline your ear: Forget your people and your father's house: Then the King will desire your beauty. Because He is your Lord, bow down to Him. The daughter of Tyre will come with a gift; The rich among the people will seek your favor. The King's daughter is all glorious within; Her clothing is interwoven with gold. She will be led to the King in embroidered work; The virgins, her companions who follow her, will be brought to You.*

You have beauty (this applies even to the men among my readers!) meant to be seen in private by

God alone, like a husband who is the only person to see his wife wearing her undergarments.

The King wants the secret place of your heart.

Chapter 22

God's Pocket

Therefore, brethren, having boldness to enter the Holiest by the blood of Jesus, by a new and living way which He consecrated for us, through the veil, that is, His flesh, and having a High Priest over the house of God, let us draw near with a true heart in full assurance of faith, having our hearts sprinkled from an evil conscience and our bodies washed with pure water.
(Hebrews 10:19-22)

I am hidden in His pocket. He tells me I am in His pocket as a rock in David's pocket when he approached that giant Goliath.

I can imagine the rocks in his pocket felt like no small pebbles. His adrenaline was pumping, and his heart was in his throat. Perhaps, he felt as though one of those stones was in his throat. The task before Him was enormous, yet uppermost in His mind was the fact that this giant had dared to challenge God. I imagine a little sweat glistening on his forehead. The stones in his pocket felt large, like the task. They burned like fire as he engaged his faith amid his fear. I do not imagine that the presence of his faith was the absence of fear; it was simple trust in the bigness of His God despite his fear.

He had faced predators before. The bear and the lion had both succumbed in their battles with David. Saul offered him his own armor, but it was too heavy; it offered David no benefit whatsoever. His only advantages were the stones in his pocket and his slingshot.

This makes me think of how often we try to apply the "strategies" of others in our warfare, as if a formula that would guarantee us a win if we just used it. But the power is not in the strategy but in the TRUST. It is not in "the name of this Jesus whom Paul knows" I cast demons out. It is not in the teachings of any celebrity Christian you might name that you are guaranteed an overcomer's life. It is by YOUR faith and experience in the name and character of God that you gain victory over your enemies.

So, what might God be saying when He impresses upon me that I am a stone in His pocket? The first thing that comes to mind is a sense of His closeness, of being inside something. To see or feel the inside of what could not be seen on the outside. He tells me sometimes we are in a spiritual "pocket" when He draws men closer to reveal Himself to them. They have a particular experience, while those around them have another. You could be standing right beside a person who is lost in the Presence of God and be completely unaware there is anything different about them.

Jesus was in this pocket in John 12:27-29.

"Now My soul has become troubled; and what shall I say, Father, save Me from this hour? But for this purpose, I came to this hour. Father, glorify Your name." Then a voice came out of heaven: "I have both glorified it and will glorify it again." So the crowd who stood by and heard it said that it had thundered; others were saying, "An angel has spoken to Him."

God's Pocket

The crowd was outside of the pocket. When Moses got closer to God, to speak to Him face to face, he entered the pocket of God's revelation. But to the crowd, it was a fearsome thing; they did not see what Moses saw.

Exodus 20:18-21 All the people heard thunder and saw the lightning flashes and the sound of the trumpet and the mountain smoking. When the people saw it, they trembled and stood at a distance. Then they said to Moses, "Speak to us yourself, and we will listen; but let not God speak to us, or we will die." Moses told the people, "Do not be afraid; for God has come in order to test you, and in order that the fear of Him may remain with you, so that you may not sin." So the people stood at a distance while Moses approached the thick cloud where God was.

Today, we do the same thing. We want others to approach God for us. We do not know enough about God's character to be secure in how He might respond to us if we try to get closer. Perhaps He is angry with us. It is far easier to let our personal Moses, our pastor, our favourite celebrity teacher, preacher, or prophetic person tell us the rules and give us a formula so that we can perform our duties without the risk of approaching God ourselves. To be in someone's pocket used to be a common idiom. It means being so close to and actively involved with someone that you know all their comings and goings. The idea is that you know everybody's business: "I'm tired of villages where everyone lives in everyone else's pocket."

What does it mean to be a rock in God's pocket? To be realistic about our size? To be aware of our stature in relation to His size and might. To choose to stay close to God, to approach Him to see Him as He is. To experience Him, let Him draw us into His Presence to experience Him for ourselves.

The rocks in David's pockets were an unlikely strategy.

We are God's unlikely strategy against His enemies on the earth.

The power is not in the strategy but in whose Hand we are in.

A small stone in the right Hand need only be used once to strike down a giant.

Chapter 23

Clark Kent

He has shown you, oh mortal, what is good. And what does the Lord require of you? To act justly and to love mercy and to walk humbly with your God.
(Micah 6:8)

In my dream, a man is in a hospital room fighting for breath but is not ill. The air is so full of beings at war that the oxygen is being squeezed out of the atmosphere. There is no oxygen to breathe in. These beings that fill the sky and his room are like clouds, but they are not and have giant faces. They are like marble and yet almost transparent. Smoke and yet I somehow see outlines of muscular arms engaged in combat. They are massive and yet without definition at the same time. It is like they are reality and there is no room for anything else to exist on their level. Their shape is defined by where they end and their cohort or their opponents begin. One is in the front, leading the way with a fiercely determined expression. I feel an urgency and call to fight; fight for our very air!

The scene changes but I know that the scene has only changed to a different battle zone of the same war as the one being waged in the hospital room. I am looking for someone I know to be a leader of the resistance in this war in the heavens. I find him and a few others, and we are discussing going to his hideout when an armed soldier arrives. The others disperse, and I am left "hiding in plain sight" in a phone booth. The soldier approaches me and points his massive gun at me, demanding that I tell him the direction the others went. He adds that he will kill me if I refuse to tell him.

I somehow manage to lose him and find the hideout. This turns out to be a house that was converted into apartments. But the walls between the different suites are made of glass and I can see everything my neighbours are doing.

I wait for the others to arrive and know I am between assignments, so I decide to bake both bread and cake. Once finished, I put everything away in the cupboards and clean all signs of my presence in the apartment so I cannot be found. However, I realize that people will know someone was there because of the smell of the baking.

The resistance leader and two others show up to give me my assignment. I am to go undercover as a cheerleader. I prepare for this assignment by bathing. I have a sense that I am being purified. A sense this was more than a bath but a purification ritual that would take me to a deeper level of surrender to God.

I wake feeling suffocated. The air is dense and close around me. I am experiencing the same thing as the man in my dream. I can feel the proximity of the cloud-like beings with the faces set like flint. My heart is pounding, my breath is short as I realize this is more than a dream. I am in the middle of an angelic visitation, and I still feel their presence and the intensity of the battle they engage in. I sense an exhortation and encouragement to be spiritually alert for days following this dream. I feel the intensity of being threatened and intimidated in my spirit. I also feel the angels on my side. A war is being waged over me, over the body of Christ. I pray in the Spirit.

When the atmosphere clears a few days later, I think about some of the puzzling aspects of the dream. I wonder why I hid in a phone booth. That seemed incongruous.

I ask the Lord," How do people hide in plain sight?" and the answer comes softly, "Humility."

I remember the phone booth is where mild-mannered Clark Kent became Superman.

It dawns on me that to clothe oneself in humility and appear unassuming is a safety posture!

Then this Scripture comes to mind.

Philippians 2: 5-8 Have this attitude in which was also in Christ Jesus, who, although He existed in the form of God, did not regard equality with God as a thing to be grasped, but emptied Himself, taking the form of a bondservant and being made in the likeness of men. Being found in appearance as a man, He humbled Himself by becoming obedient to the point of death, even death on a cross.

I could hear the Lord saying He gives us victory over our enemies through humility. The fact that the walls of the hideout were made of glass re-iterates this theme. What comes to mind is the old adage: Those who live in glass houses should not throw stones." We must function as we would if our secret sins were visible to those around us, all too aware of our need for mercy.

I feel a need to research the verses about the faces of flint.

Jeremiah 5:3 "Oh Lord, you are looking for faithfulness; you have tried to get them to be honest, for you Have punished them, but they will not change. You destroy them, but they refuse to turn from their sins. They are determined with faces as hard as flint not to repent."

Isaiah 50:7 "For the Lord God helps Me. Therefore, I am not disgraced; Therefore, I have set My face like flint, And I know that I will not be ashamed."

This was a prophecy about Jesus. He had set His face like flint towards Jerusalem, towards the cross, and because of this, He won the victory. I became burdened for repentance in the body of Christ.

Oh Lord, give us respect for you, great love for you so that we will WANT to be more submitted to you with our faces set like flint toward OBEDIENCE to you instead of turning away from you, continuing in our sin; living in grace but lacking in power! The reason for the bath, the cleansing ritual is there is a higher level of surrender needed to bring a higher level of victory to bring healing and deliverance to others.

In this time of increased warfare, the Lord reminds us that our strategy should be humility and obedience. Grace does not cancel the need to obey. As the Lord conquers us, we conquer the land. When He is victorious over us, and when He is truly our Lord. we get the victory.

Prov 16:32 He who is slow to anger is better than the mighty, And he who rules his spirit than he who captures a city.

Chapter 24

Intercessors Wanted

Oh! the depths of the riches both of the wisdom and knowledge of God! How unsearchable are His judgments, and His ways past finding out! "For who has known the mind of the LORD or who has become His counselor? Or who has first given to Him that it might be repaid to Him?" For of Him and through Him and to Him are all things, to whom be glory forever. Amen. (Romans 11:33-36)

*F*irst Corinthians 13:32 "The spirit of the prophets is subject to the prophets" is used today to claim that uncontrollable manifestations are not of God. People believe that being mystical equals being flaky, and there is no room for anything but that which is restrained and what is deemed dignified. But manifestations still happen; travail, uncontrollable weeping, moaning, and groaning, and shaking are all found in the Bible.

I talk to another intercessor friend, and during our conversation, I can hear the hunger to understand and to be understood in her role in the big picture of the dynamics of church life. The body of Christ has a limited understanding of the experiences of prophetic intercessors. Congregations want us to pray but show little curiosity about how such intercession works. Many do not value it enough to have the patience to learn. If we would just go into a closet—where no one would be bothered by the uncomfortable manifestations—and still get answers to prayer, all the better.

I find it difficult sometimes to physically handle the power of the Spirit. The Bible tells us the Spirit is a well of Living Water. He has a life of His own! At times, the power is being held back by a dam. When it releases senses are overwhelmed and there does not seem to be time to gain self control, or an opportunity to control the intensity. We may not know why people weep uncontrollably, travail, or physically shake, or exactly HOW it is connected to the growth of the kingdom of God, so why should we allow it?

But it is connected! And sometimes we have a problem with it.

But that does not mean we should stop it. Does it say in Scripture that we understand all things? Does it mean that if we don't understand something, it can't be from God? His move is limited by our understanding.

I'm sorry, but that sounds like the attitude and demeanor of the Pharisees.

We must study to show ourselves approved in the things of God, absolutely.

We must submit our experiences to the counsel of Scripture and make it our plumbline. Of course!

There is much to learn. And Jesus promised to leave the Holy Spirit to lead us into all truth. We must hold both Spirit and truth as necessary and vital.

We need to be students of the Word, and humble disciples open to the things of the Spirit.

We should not be rigid allowing only our understanding of what the Scriptures say, instead of what it says. The Bible tells us we should be transformed by renewing your mind. This happens by the suspension of our own agenda. We should be open to be taught. I heard someone say, "You don't know everything, and you are not always right!" A hearty amen to that from my corner!

To understand the reference about the "renewal of the mind," which is from Romans 12:2, we must know the verb tense used to accurately translate this phrase. "Be transformed" is an imperative present tense and might more accurately state, "be being transformed or keep being transformed by the continual or ongoing renewal of your mind." Be in a constant state of growing in the grace and knowledge of God.

My heart goes out to the prophetic intercessors who have been misunderstood and rejected because of their Spirit-led expressions in the church. If you are an intercessor with these experiences, please do not isolate yourself.

You are needed and vital to the body of Christ. Intercessors are like the liver of the body—the liver filters all the blood in the body and breaks down poisonous substances. The liver also produces bile, which helps digest fats and carry away waste. Intercessors are often the first people in the church to experience the strategy of the enemy because God reveals it to them. He is preparing them to be a source of strength when the rest of the body goes through it.

Intercessors, you are our lifeblood. We need you.

Remain connected to the body!

Chapter 25

Ship Out Of Water

And to the angel of the church in Sardis write, "These things says He who has the seven Spirits of God and the seven stars: "I know your works, that you have a name that you are alive, but you are dead. Be watchful, and strengthen the things which remain, that are ready to die, for I have not found your works perfect before God. Remember therefore how you have received and heard; hold fast and repent. Therefore if you will not watch, I will come upon you as a thief, and you will not know what hour I will come upon you."
(Revelation 3:1-3)

I dream I am taking a tour of a ship. A colourful character of a captain is taking me through, describing its best attributes. He is somewhat like Captain Hook. He is wearing a long red velvet jacket and pants with a white shirt and purple vest. His facial features are large and animated. His demeanor is quite jovial. I hit my hand against the vessel's wall as if testing to see what it is made of. Then a weird thing happens. In my mind's eye, my perspective pans out to a wide-angle view of the ship, and I can see that it is not real but a sand sculpture on the beach! I pat the wall again and say, "Land ahoy!"

The captain laughs.

"It is not a ship. It only looks like one," I say, and he responds, "That is the beauty of it." Complete safety! The illusion of adventure! At first, I felt comfort of it and thought, what a clever idea! But it is not a real ship. It cannot go anywhere!

And the safety begins to feel suffocating, like a coffin.

I wake up knowing the meaning of the dream.

The ship is the church. The church wants to be safe.

The church prioritizes appearances over taking risks. It does not matter what we DO, whether we set out to sea or not, but just what it LOOKS like we are doing. There is no life.

This saddens me and gives me an urgency to pray.

Now is not the time to point the finger, criticizing the church as some of us do—as if we are not a part of it! I am too aware of my shortcomings to find fault. It is time to identify with a church that is more afraid than alive to God. I know I have my ways in which I resist God.

The cry for God's intervention starts to rise within me. I experience physical pain as I cry out, "Oh Lord, come make us real."

Like the Velveteen Rabbit[1], we need to be loved into a visceral experience of life. We must be conversant with the life of God in us! We have an appearance of life but are dead! The same Spirit that raised Christ from the dead lives in us! The world could be vastly different if the church manifested the life of Christ *en masse*.

---

1   *The Velveteen Rabbit*, by Marjery Williams, 1920. Wikipedia states: "A stuffed rabbit sewn from velveteen is given as a Christmas present to a small boy. The boy plays with his other new presents and forgets the velveteen rabbit for a time. These presents are modern and mechanical, and they snub the old-fashioned velveteen rabbit. The wisest and oldest toy in the nursery, the Skin Horse, which was owned by the boy's uncle, tells the rabbit (whom he feels sorry for) about toys being made Real by love of children: 'Real isn't how you are made... It's a thing that happens to you.'"

The only hope is for each of us to die to self and become alive to God individually. We are only we are experiencing a fraction of what is possible in the Spirit!

I groan in intercession, and a Scripture verse comes to mind.

Galatians 4:19 Oh, my dear children! I feel as if I'm going through labor pains for you again, and they will continue until Christ is fully developed in your lives.

My body experiences the labour pains, and I pray with urgency. I sense the opposition of the enemy in our lives. He is fighting against the Kingdom of God being manifested. Of course, he doesn't want us abiding in the life and power of the Risen Christ!

I feel the level of the living water in the well in my spirit rise. A glimmer of hope vibrates in my chest, which begins to hurt. Labour again overtakes me. I pray and rock my body as I press in for the answer to that prayer for the life of Christ to be formed in the church.

Let everything that raises itself against the knowledge (experience) of God be broken down.

Now! Dry bones come to life! Holy Spirit, fill Your body with Your breath!

I sing "Spirit Break Out" by William McDowell:

Spirit break out
Break our walls down

Spirit break out
Heaven come down…

I am filled with assurance the Lord hears me.

He has given me this prayer, and He will answer it.

Thank You, Lord.

It is time to be heartened to put out to sea until we "see" a navy of ships heading out of the harbour.

Chapter 26

Honour

Then I looked, and I heard
the voice of many angels
around the throne,
the living creatures,
and the elders;
and the number of them
was ten thousand times ten thousand,
and thousands of thousands, saying
with a loud voice: "Worthy is the lamb
who was slain to receive power and
riches and wisdom, and strength and
honor and glory and blessing!"
(Revelation 5:11-12)

I dream I am in a small room behind the stage of a stadium. I'm with people who will be performing there.

One of the women puts on a blue velvet and white chiffon gown, and goes onto the stage where she is then lifted into the air as if she is flying. It turns out she is being carried around the stadium, mosh pit style, in the upraised arms of the crowd that is gathered there.

The members of our group take turns wearing the gown and flying over the crowd, one after the other. But there is a big problem. Each of us who wears the dress, after their turn to be lifted, randomly attacks people to bite them as if hungry! Yet no one seems bothered by it.

My turn comes, and I forget my concern and allow myself to be lifted. I cannot believe how wonderful it feels! It is truly like flying! I circle the stadium twice, being held up on the hands and arms of others.

I wake up with a feeling of euphoria. How wonderful it feels to be lifted like that.

As I begin the day, I ponder the various elements of the dream and wonder what they mean. The colour and material of the dress, the performers, and the fact that it was being filmed. And why were we biting other people after our turn in the air?

Sometimes dream interpretation principles are not always about the details.

Sometimes, you are to pay attention to a whisper in your spirit when you sit down to record a dream. It may be completely different than dream symbology will try to explain. The whisper I hear as I write today is this phrase:

How can you believe when you receive glory from one another?

John 5:41-44 "I do not receive glory from men; but I know you, that you do not have the love of God in yourselves. I have come in My Father's name, and you do not receive Me; if another comes in his own name, you will receive him. How can you believe when you receive glory from one another and do not seek the glory from the one and only God?"

I instantly think of the crowds in my dream. They were raising us on their uplifted arms.

The meaning seemed to leap out at me. It symbolized receiving glory, the lifting up of man.

Contemporary synonyms for glory are honour, praise, reasonable opinion, or judgment. When we glorify men, we do not believe in God. How is that? We subtract God from the equation if we exalt a person on his own merit. We do not worship God, who made man, we worship the man. We do not discern or acknowledge that God is the source of all the good gifts that make our success possible.

When we take God out of the equation, we get into trouble. We become proud or jealous of another person's success. *They got the recognition, and I didn't, and I am just as worthy as them.* We bite and chew one another (Galatians 5:15)

When we take God out of the equation, we develop our own system of standards for success. Based on the elements of that system, we judge people as "heroes or zeros." We have our own ways of judging whether successful or not; therefore, God's judgments don't matter. God's values don't matter. All that matters is how high I am in the "pecking order."

This is one of the main reasons the religious order of His day did not accept Jesus. They did not glorify God because He did not fit into their value system. He wasn't playing by their rules. They could NOT recognize Him as coming from God. He did not fit inside their box.

When the church has a culture of valuing men too highly, we do what is called recognizing people after the flesh and not the spirit. By receiving "glory" we get either arrogant or angry and jealous when other people are promoted. This is the crux of the problem.

Galatians 5:13-15 For you were called to freedom,

> *brethren; only do not turn your freedom into an opportunity for the flesh, but through love serve one another. For the whole Law is fulfilled in one word, in the statement, "You shall love your neighbor as yourself." But if you bite and devour one another, take care that you are not consumed by one another.*

Imagine a culture where we believed in God's evaluation as the source of worth.

In that case, we might not be so tempted by pride, jealousy, and strife—antonyms for servanthood as prescribed in the earlier reference.

> *1 Corinthians 3:3 …for you, are still fleshly. Since there is jealousy and strife among you, are you not fleshly, and are you not walking like mere men when you receive glory from one another?*

> *James 3:16-17 For where jealousy and selfish ambition exist, there is disorder and every evil thing. 17 But the wisdom from above is first pure, then peaceable, gentle, reasonable, full of mercy, and good fruits, unwavering, without hypocrisy.*

So then, let us not consider people as worthy of exaltation nor disparage them as "nobody."

Let us love each other but give glory only to One.

Chapter 27

Do You Want to be Important?

...but, speaking the truth in love, may grow up in all things into Him who is the head—Christ— from whom the whole body, joined and knit together by what every joint supplies, according to the effective working by which every part does its share, causes growth of the body for the edifying of itself in love.
(Ephesians 4:15-16)

I dream a camera is doing a close-up of a female cartoon face. Big red lips. Big hair. Big eyelashes. Big everything, ha! The camera zooms out, revealing that this face is attached to the front of the wing of a plane. It starts talking. "I AM A WING!" the face boasts.

"The plane does not go anywhere without me! But WITH me? I take you higher; I can take you to places you could not go before! With me, you can see from a higher viewpoint. You can go longer distances! With me, you can even go to different countries!"

The camera slowly continues to pull out, and you see that the boastful wing is not attached to a plane!

Then the camera rolls back farther, and you see this little wing is by itself in a hangar.

Unfortunately, we prophetic folk can be like this wing—proud of ourselves and our gifting. Aware, shall we say, of the possibilities of our capabilities.

Guess what? You are useless if you are not attached.

The body is built up by that which every joint supplies. EVERY joint. Who or what do we supply?

THE BODY. If you are prophetic, you need to be supplying the body. We are as useless as a wing without being attached to a plane.

Sure, I can see your potential. Yes, that was an impressive revelation! God DOES speak to you powerfully; you have an incredible gift. You have POTENTIAL! That is right, potential, and it is a meaningless waste until you function in a way that improves the lives of others.

Sometimes, we think that we must be important to be significant. "Important" means to be special in and of myself.

Significance speaks to my contribution to others.

When God gave me this dream, it blew my pride.

I thought I was "all that."

If we work together, we go places.

Because we do not, we **cannot**, do it ALONE.

Chapter 28

The Necklace

Now the word of the Lord came to Samuel, saying, "I greatly regret that I have set up Saul as king, for he has turned back from following Me, and has not performed My commandments." And it grieved Samuel, and he cried out to the Lord all night. So when Samuel rose early in the morning to meet Saul, it was told Samuel, saying, "Saul went to Carmel, and indeed, he set up a monument for himself; and he has gone on around, passed by, and gone down to Gilgal."
(1 Samuel 15:10-12)

In my dream I am wandering through a public market, with booths selling food, clothing, jewelry, spices, and everything else one might want. I am myself, in my own attire, but the dream is set in biblical times. Other people are wearing Middle Eastern attire, and the town square is full of tents arranged along dusty streets. I walk with one hand in front of me, gripping a necklace. I am solely focused on that necklace, protecting it as if holding it is safer than wearing it. I can scan the crowd nervously and am prepared to fight anyone who might try to take it from me. My hands are sweaty as I clutch the gold chain with a large pink coral pendant. I held it so tightly because it had been given to me by the Lord. It was a symbol, not only of his love but I understood it to be a token of authority. It was God jewelry so to speak. It was my Proverbs 25 necklace.

Proverbs 25: 11-12 A word fitly spoken is like apples of gold in pictures of silver. As an earring of gold, and an ornament of fine gold, so is a wise reprover upon an obedient ear.

At this point, a young boy approaches me. He is only around twelve years old but there is an air of sophistication or wisdom around him. How can someone so young have a commanding presence? But he did. Commanding yet approachable.

"You are supposed to wear it," he says, reaching toward me, and for some reason I let him gently take it from my hand. Walking behind me, he fastens the chain around my neck. I immediately feel free from the fear that someone could take it.

"The necklace is meant to be worn, not held in your hand like a trophy someone might steal." His words are soft, but His eyes penetrate mine. So much is contained in that look!

He understands my insecurity and fear and how I prize this token of His favour.

Joy fills my heart; I can wear it and forget it. I can walk like I own it!

Are you not tempted, at times, to cling to a revelation God gives you in just such a way? You seek to hang on to it jealously as if it validates your self-worth. When you hear Him speak to you, do you think He loves you, but when you don't hear Him, perhaps He is angry with you?

God speaks to us not because we are especially worthy in a way others are not. He speaks to us because He loves us and that can not be taken from us.

We are not to hold on so tightly to our own revelation of God that we can't receive revelations He gives others. We must allow what He tells us to have its effect, to beautify us. At the same time, we must not fear losing it. We must wear it. Meaning we must embody the word not just hear it and prize it.

The bride is cleansed, made whole, and beautified by the revelation He gives each one of us.

While clinging to the necklace like that, my hand could not be used to do something else! Of course, the young boy in my dream was Jesus. He was going about His Father's business while His mother was looking for Him all around the marketplace.

If the necklace represents prophetic revelation, what are we to understand about it from the perspective of this pure young man? He was going about doing good, living in the Father's purpose of each moment. He advised, "Wear it and forget it; don't wear it like a badge. We don't have to cling to it as if it is the only sign of his favor, as if He will not give us anything else. When we allow the power of the Word affect our actions, we become the word.

Let other people look at it all they want without fear that anything they say might have the power to take it away. Don't obsess about it or guard it jealously.

You just want to get about your father's business. Secure in his love. His speaking to you is not the definition of his favor but a reflection of his magnanimous character that we can trust and abide in.

Chapter 29

Singing Servant

In that day it shall be said to Jerusalem: "Do not fear; Zion, let not your hands be weak. The Lord your God in your midst, The Mighty One, will save; He will rejoice over you with gladness, He will quiet you with His love, He will rejoice over you with singing."
(Zephaniah 3:16-17)

*I*n *my dream*, it is someone's birthday, and my neighbor has removed his fence so we can have the whole yard for a party. I am excited and trying to wake my daughter up so she can attend the party. She is young and cranky and does not want to leave her bed. Few people are there, so the neighbors invite us into their house. Others follow, and the party now takes over the whole home. It is jubilant, rowdy even. At one point, we decide to make a video of one of the guests. She is an older woman dressed in white and pearls. It seems like she is a bride, but she is wearing a nightgown instead of a bridal gown. She stands in front of a mirror and leans forward to cover her face and neck in fine white powder.

She starts singing in another language, strong-voiced and powerful. Someone hands her a baby to sing over. Somehow, I know the baby does not whave a name. Time seems to stand still as she sings. All eyes are on the old woman and the child.

Eventually, the party ends.

The guests leave, and everyone who lives in the house goes to bed. I feel like an interloper, but I stay as if waiting for something. Eventually, I hear a man moving around upstairs, and after a moment he comes down, preparing to leave for work. I quickly make myself busy cleaning up the place, picking up dirty glasses, and singing the tune the older woman in white had sung.

It is now daylight; I feel a little awkward being there; almost as if I had been caught spying. So I continue to busy myself cleaning.

I feel like I am still in the dream when I wake up. All I can see in my mind is the older woman. I feel like I know her and even feel the essence of her character; her presence is with me!

For three days, all I can do is pray in tongues. The second night, I woke up saying, "It would be foolish to give the baby a name now."

I ask the Lord the identity of older woman in the dream. Does she represent the Holy Spirit, or is she an angel? Or will I meet her one day?

And He says, "She is you. I am giving you an assignment. I will cause you to be a wise woman" (pearls are equated with wisdom in Scripture) "who watches over and sings over the baby" (the Church) "in the night watches" (nightgown, cleaning up when others are asleep).

I am to sing in a heavenly language over the new life of the Church that does not yet have a name. I am to sing a new song over her in tongues. I am to be an unassuming, singing servant in the night watches.

Singing Servant

Psalm 119:147-148 I rise before dawn and cry for help; I wait for Your words. My eyes anticipate the night watches, So that I may meditate on Your word.

Know this, dear reader, that it does not matter whether anyone knows what you are doing in the Lord's name.

Just do it!

Chapter 30

One Last Dream

Now it came to pass
as He sat at the table with them,
that He took bread,
blessed and broke it,
and gave it to them.
Then their eyes were opened,
then they knew Him;
and He vanished from their sight.
And they said to one another,
"Did not our hearts burn within us
while He talked with us on the road
and while He opened the Scriptures to us?"
(Luke 24: 30-32)

I just had the most beautiful dream.

I saw a young woman and everywhere she went, she brought laughter and joy—*joie de vivre*, the joy of life. She was intent on "being in the present."

If you met her, you were tremendously lucky. You were very blessed because she brought you to life. Everywhere she went she brought things to life. There were little pods of people in the places she travelled who had become her friends. They could not wait until the next time she would suddenly appear in their lives, and for a while they would all feel alive. Together.

Sometimes she travelled with a friend, but mostly, she was alone. A film crew planned to make a movie about her. Like the TV show "Friends." The movie would highlight each character impacted by the young woman and how they had all gotten connected because of her. There was so much love—thick love in the atmosphere of the dream.

The young woman is you, is me. She is also a picture of Christ. And we, the whole bride of Christ is to be like her. Bringing people to life wherever we go. Her friends somehow found out there was only going to be one more message from her, and then they would never see her again. So, they were creating music, poetry, and lots (and lots) of good food. They did not know what day or time they were going get the message, so they were busy preparing, each person doing something that she had brought to life in them. From the youngest—two young boys—to a very elderly couple, I saw all different ages, all different kinds of people. United by only one thing: the young woman. People were in the living room talking about her, telling stories about her. One story made one of the women hungry, and she reached into some shelves behind her. Two shelves up was a cake and she took it down to eat it.

I heard a voice cry out, "No that's for later!" She said "Oh I got so hungry because she was talking about food!" And everyone laughed. It needs to be said that there is something about people talking about their personal experience with God. It makes us hungry for that. Like the disciples on the road to Emmaus, time with the risen Jesus made their hearts burn. It satisfies while at the same time makes us hungry for more!

Suddenly a TV in the living room sparked to life and there she was, her back to the camera, on the phone, engaged in a lively conversation. She realized the camera was on her and hung up, then turned around with the brightest, most radiant smile of joy, and she sat down on a big white and rose-coloured stuffed armchair. She gracefully leaned forward, her eyes sparkling with anticipation, alive with passion, and proceeded to begin her last message.

I heard someone say, "Stop it, stop it! I want to hear it from the beginning!"

And so, they did. They rewound the tape. They wanted to be together to catch every word.

To me this was a picture of what happened in the upper room. Jesus promised He would send His Spirit to be with them. I do not think they knew what to expect. Did they wonder if Jesus would walk through the wall again? Would one of them receive a word or direction in a trance? All they knew was the one who had brought them to life, who had the words of life, who Himself had died and rose again had promised. He had promised in John 16 to send the Spirit of truth to tell them everything they would need to know.

I am sure they were full of anticipation. All of them excited to be together to experience what Jesus promised. When we gather today, do we come with as much anticipation? With open yielded and expectant hearts?

Chapter 31

The Sand

"But as for me, I would seek God,
And to God I would commit my cause—
Who does great things, and unsearchable,
Marvelous things without number."
(Job 5:8-9)

And there are also many other things
that Jesus did, which if they were written
one by one,
I suppose that even the world itself
could not contain the books
that would be written. Amen.

Psalm 139:17-18 How precious also are Your thoughts for me, God! How vast is the sum of them! Were I to count them, they would outnumber the sand. When I awake, I am still with You.

*T*his collection of my experiences with God has been like a child playing with a pail and shoveling in the sand on the great expanse of God's thoughts toward us.

He speaks in so many ways. The father of many children communicates differently with each of them because each is different. The children need different things from their father. He speaks to them in a way that will touch those needs.

You can see that the heavenly Father speaks to me frequently in dreams. I understand things more clearly with a visual example of what is being said.

A picture is worth a thousand words. Jesus used this method in teaching through parables.

He related truth in ways that His hearers could easily understand.

I hope reading this book has given you a taste of the sweetness of the tone of voice I hear from the Lord. His love is tender toward us!

Because He loves us, the Lord also corrects us. He points out where our thinking is not in line with His character, as revealed in Scripture. He is faithful.

I pray that this small opportunity to see God through another's eyes has given you a view you may not have experienced previously. I pray that you hear and feel His love for you in a fresh way.

God bless you in your journey to discover Him who is the pearl of great price.

www.ingramcontent.com/pod-product-compliance
Lightning Source LLC
Chambersburg PA
CBHW060526080526
44586CB00012B/632